100 Questions to Ask Your Software Organization

First Edition

Mark I. Himelstein

Copyright © 2005 by Heavenstone, Inc.

All rights reserved. No part of this book shall be reproduced or transmitted in any form or by any means, electronic, mechanical, magnetic, photographic including photocopying, recording or by any information storage and retrieval system, without prior written permission of the publisher. No patent liability is assumed with respect to the use of the information contained herein. Although every precaution has been taken in the preparation of this book, the publisher and author assume no responsibility for errors or omissions. Neither is any liability assumed for damages resulting from the use of the information contained herein.

Editors: Sandra Himelstein and Tony Barreca

Cover Art: ©1996 Ian Coleman. All Rights Reserved. Reproduced with permission from Ian Coleman.

Trademarks: Six Sigma is a registered trademark of Motorola Inc. IPlanet, Java, Solaris, and SunOS are trademarks of Sun Microsystems Inc., Microsoft and PivotTable are registered trademarks of Microsoft Corporation. ISO is a registered trademark of the International Organization for Standardization, Fortune 500 is a registered trademark of Time Incorporated.

ISBN 0-7414-2739-7

Published by:

1094 New DeHaven Street, Suite 100
West Conshohocken, PA 19428-2713
Info@buybooksontheweb.com
www.buybooksontheweb.com
Toll-free (877) BUY BOOK
Local Phone (610) 941-9999
Fax (610) 941-9959

Printed in the United States of America

Printed on Recycled Paper

Published September 2006

Table of Contents

Introduction i
Chapter 1: Communication 1
    No Surprises 2
    Escalations 5
    Rationale 8
    Venues 9
    Consensus 11
    Messages and Rules 12
    Managing Up 17
Chapter 2: Roles and Responsibilities 19
    One Owner 20
    Matrix Organizations 22
    Steering 25
    Program Management 27
    Quality Assurance 29
    Information vs. Decisions 30
    Delegation 32
    Accountability 33
    Identifying Roles 34
    Separation 36

Table Of Contents

- Chapter 3: Strategy 39
  - Engineer's Lament 40
  - Elevator Pitch 41
  - Context and Organization 42
- Chapter 4: Resources 47
  - Budgets 48
  - Hiring 52
  - Layoffs 56
- Chapter 5: Schedules 58
  - Form versus Function 59
  - Granularity and Milestones 61
- Chapter 6: Execution 66
  - Auditing progress 67
  - Continuous Improvement 69
  - Marketing Yourself and Your Group 71
- Chapter 7: Development Processes 74
  - Processes 75
  - Criteria 76
  - Source code control 78
  - Release Models 80
  - Managing Bugs 81
- Chapter 8: Remote Management 85
  - Why Do It? 86
  - Center of Gravity 87
  - Care and Feeding 88
  - How to Do It 89
- Chapter 9: Offshoring 92
  - Why Do It? 93

Table of Contents

Chapter 10: Humanity 95
    Make Them Feel Heard 96
    Accomplishment 97
    Reviews 98
    Success 101
    Do the Right Thing 101
    Compensation 102
    Empathy 105

Chapter 11: Final Words 107

Appendix: Project Example 108
    Elevator Pitch 109
    Owners 109
    Budget Categories 111
    Reliability Strategy 112
    Budgets 121
    Project Proposal 125
    Criteria Document 135
    Schedule 138

Index of Questions 147

Acknowledgments 154

About The Author 155

Introduction

I never had aspirations to become a manager.

I became a manager for the first time over twenty years ago and I had no clue as to what it meant. I had been an organized and productive engineer, and they gave me the role in the hope that I could help others become organized and productive. My groups succeeded in their tasks only because of my prowess as an individual programmer. I was a failure as a manager.

I went back and forth from individual contributor to manager a number of times until thirteen years later when I took the leap for good. Even then they asked me if I would rather pursue the engineering ladder as a distinguished engineer or pursue management. I answered that I felt I could help the company more in management. I never looked back.

I manage because I know I have skills and experience that can help companies and people succeed. I do it because I enjoy producing products that customers want to use and because I enjoy building successful organizations.

This book is a how-to-guide that will shorten your journey to both understanding and effectively leading a software organization. It is organized by questions you could and should ask your teams. The book also provides real answers and guidance based on my experience.

Just as in painting a house, there is a lot of preparation required to create an effective organization that can produce quality products on time and meet customer needs. The chapters on *Communication*, *Roles* and *Responsibilities,* and *Strategy* lay that foundation. Then there are practical matters around *Resources*, *Schedules*, *Development Processes,* and *Execution* that provide basic instruction on how to proceed with building a product. Chapters are provided on handling *Remote Sites* and *Offshoring* – both of which have become incredibly critical in today's world. Finally, I include a chapter on *Humanity* touching on issues that encourage loyalty and provide job satisfaction.

The book's narrative is targeted at software managers, but everyone from software developers, software managers, executives who have software groups reporting to them, and investors in software companies can benefit from this book. It provides both insight into the software process and practical information that will help you succeed. I believe that the techniques in this book scale and can be useful in all sizes and complexities of organizations.

My credentials include working in startups (Megatest, Inc., MIPS, Inc., Digeo, Inc., and Infoblox, Inc.), my own consulting firms: Heavenstone, Inc. and Himelsoft, Inc., and in larger corporations (Sandia Corp., Apple Computer, Inc., and Sun Microsystems Inc.). I have a track record of building teams and delivering products with quality and on time. I describe myself as an executionist capable of helping teams and companies succeed. I hope that this book helps you in your job as a software manager, executive, developer, or even investor.

I have had my successes and my failures. I am also writing this book for myself because it is easy to forget some of these items no matter how experienced you are. I have strengths and areas for improvement like anyone else. I hope that I can impart both in this book. One note on format: section and chapter references are in italics.

The Greeks said, "Everything in moderation." If it were easy, they wouldn't have had to say it. I am very direct throughout the book. It is important that you apply moderation and judgment when using ideas from this book in your situation

Writing words,

Mark I. Himelstein

Chapter 1: Communication

This chapter describes some of the basics of how to communicate as a manager. Communication is the number one quality I look for in prospective employees. Rather than go into how to communicate well (there are a lot of books on that topic), I concentrate on fundamentals of communicating within Software Development Groups.

The chapter addresses items that are important in managing up (your manager and up), down (your employees and down), and sideways (your peers). It starts with a keystone for communication in any business with the section on *No Surprises* and goes on to talk a lot about actual techniques to communicate in your organization including how to handle *Escalations*, in what *Venues* to communicate, taking the time to explain *Rationale*, and some words on *Consensus* building. Finally, I provide a discussion on the major tools at your disposal with a section on *Message and Rules* and a section on the process of *Managing Up*.

No Surprises

> *1. Do you get critical information in a timely manner?*

I have one rule on which I am very strict and that is: "No surprises".

You will see throughout this book that communication is king. This may be intuitive and obvious, but it is easy to forget when you are in the tough part of a project and incredibly busy.

When I am introduced as the new leader of an organization, my first comment to employees is the rule stated above: I expect no surprises.

Here are some examples of surprises:

- Learning that a schedule will be missed at the end of a development cycle.
- Learning from a product manager that an employee got angry and yelled at someone instead of the manager of the employee reporting to you.
- Learning from the CEO (instead of your engineer) that a customer had an installation problem while a developer was at the site.
- Learning that an employee is leaving the company on their last day even though they gave two weeks notice.

Your employees may surprise you for a variety of reasons including:

- Believing things will get better and trying to wait until they get better before reporting an issue.
- Believing that they can address the issues themselves and not wanting to inform or involve management.
- Avoiding reporting an issue because they are embarrassed.
- Resisting an approved plan because they have their own agenda.

- Not communicating with each other and not even knowing some problems are occurring.

The more time you have to solve a problem, the more options you may have. You have more flexibility to trade off or help your employee make a tradeoff between things like features and schedule. You can only do so if you have the information.

> **2. Have you established a culture that encourages addressing tough issues?**

Problems are just things you get to solve together with your team. The corollary to "No Surprises" is that you should not kill the messenger unless he or she is three weeks late in providing the information (although kill is never the correct term!). People are scared to share information at times. Previous managers might have taught them that they will only get grief for sharing hard or bad news.

Each manager must extend himself or herself in a lot of different ways and venues. Not all people communicate the same way. Some communicate best by email or phone messages, others in one-on-one meetings, and yet others over a beer. You have to take the time to reach out and give people the chance to share.

You also have to show by example that you appreciate information. This includes active listening to show that you heard them and being polite and thanking them for coming to you. In addition, you must follow up. If someone shares information, it should not matter whether you decide to act on it or not; you need to show that you value that person by sharing what decisions you made.

I attribute the words "No surprises" to Mike Chow with whom I worked at Apple in the mid-1990's. I remember that there were a lot of behind-the-scenes discussions and intrigue, and those words were part of his efforts to bring things out into the open. Later I also saw a small mention of it in the popular book The One Minute Manager[1].

Live by the "No Surprises" rule in interacting with all the people with whom you work. No one likes surprises. It does not matter if you are communicating with your boss or your peers or your employees. Set an example and communicate everything you can.

There are times when your company may ask you to make changes that significantly affect your group. This is also a good time when you should exercise "No Surprises" as completely as you can. It is important to let people know what you are doing. Obviously, there are times when you respect confidentiality for legal reasons and for propriety's sake, but in general the rule holds.

One great example occurred when I was working at Apple and one of my groups had its budget cut. Unfortunately things were in flux, and the company would not allow me to redeploy or lay them off. This went on for three months. The situation would not have been so bad if the news of the budget cut had been kept quiet, but other folks in the company had been told. In fact my group was denied support from other groups in the company when they needed to work with those folks since we were not funded.

I could have kept things secret from the team and then they would have found out from other parts of the company. Instead, I employed "No Surprises". I was very clear and honest with my group. I told them that if they wanted to look for other jobs, they could and I would write references for them; but if they wanted to stay, I would continue to fight for them. In the end, we were funded and only two people out of 30 moved on.

---

[1] Kenneth Blanchard and Spencer Johnson, *The One Minute Manager* (New York, NY: A Berkley Book published by arrangement with William Morrow and Company, Inc., 1982), p 26.

> 3. Do people surprise you outside your organization with information regarding your organization that you did not know?

Here is another great example about surprises: one of my employees was responsible for tracking box failures with our contract manufacturer. He did not follow up with the manufacturer on some specific failures, and our contract manufacturer did not follow up with us independently. When we had our fifth failure in two months, I was surprised that my employee did not follow through on the failures until they were addressed. I was surprised that I heard about this from someone outside my organization before hearing it from my employee. I was surprised that our contract manufacturer did not follow up with us on those issues.

In the end this caused a lot of problems. Our customers saw more failures. Our support team panicked. Bad feelings arose with our support team and with our contract manufacturer. By just communicating in a more timely and effective manner, we could have quickly and easily addressed the issue. Please see the section on *Accountability* as it further addresses issues like this.

Escalations

> 4. Have you established clear escalation paths and processes?

Do not be afraid to involve management in resolving conflicts or issues.

Escalation is a term used in many places in our industry to refer to the process of raising an issue with one's management. Although this may only involve one employee, many times this occurs when employees are in disagreement and cannot come to a resolution themselves.

Escalations are just a way to ask for help. Software developers frequently do not want to ask for help. Many who become developers chose their careers because they are problem solvers. Also, we are taught independence from the moment we enter school. Most of us are not schooled in how to work together and make use of others.

It is part of a manager's job to handle escalations. Here is guidance you can give to employees regarding escalations: try to engage someone twice on an issue and if you can't get to resolution because of conflict or because they won't pay attention, escalate.

Too many times, people ruin working relationships because they try to work things out themselves. With a little help they can get to resolution and get guidance on how they should resolve conflicts in the future so they do not have to escalate. For example, I once had to merge two development teams that were working on two products that performed the same function. We were only going to continue doing one of the two and the teams could not agree about which to choose; so I asked the two architects for the two teams to present the choices and pros and cons of each choice. We had a meeting with the leaders of both teams and made a decision. Although the group who developed the product we did not choose was not happy, they felt the process was fair and that we were all part of one team.

There was another interesting situation that I experienced at one company. We had brought in a contractor to do product management for one of our products. An engineering director, who reported to me, felt that the contractor came in and tried to change how we do everything (like processes for approval of special releases and not keeping management in the loop), and that product management was not coherent about priorities (choices always have to be made). My director was visibly upset and did not know what to do. He tried email and then he tried to talk to the product management contractor directly and the discussion disintegrated.

He escalated to me and I had a talk with the contractor's boss. The contractor's manager had a totally different view of things than I did. He thought things were just fine; and if they weren't, the two opposing sides should just work it out. He told me that all of his product managers had been complaining that engineering was a block and they couldn't get anything from us. I asked why he didn't tell me about this issue prior to this discussion at the time he heard about it. He told me he would rather let his folks work it out. In the meantime, two things were occurring:

- The permanent relationship between engineering and product management was suffering.
- Things were not getting done.

If he had just sent me an email with a heads up, I could have talked to my staff about the issue. I would have ensured the problem got addressed. We could have short-circuited the escalating conflict. We would have preserved the working relationship for the next interactions.

When you set up any working relationship that requires two groups that may have different priorities or leaders, it is always useful to define the escalation path.

> **5. Have you made it clear when to escalate a problem?**

When I took the reigns of the steering committee that drove the Solaris™ product, any project that wanted to be included in Solaris came to that committee. If the committee rejected a project or required changes, all sorts of issues arose. Groups complained about the committee just being a roadblock and about not knowing what the process was. They would sometimes complain to the CEO. Sometimes verbal battles occurred in the committee. Bad feelings ensued and working relationships deteriorated.

When I revamped the procedures, processes, and committees to approve projects and programs and strategies, I set up escalation paths. If you didn't like what a committee decided or the committee couldn't decide, there was a standard escalation path. Everyone knew the rules. There was no need to duke it out. No one is ever happy when their project is rejected, but they knew there was recourse if they felt it was important enough to question the committee's judgment.

One interesting mechanism to help build the team is to require both sides of a conflict to present the issue together, presenting both sides with pros and cons. This makes things more objective and less emotional. It also makes it easier to come to a conclusion.

One comment on frequency is that some people will abuse the system and make everything an escalation. This slows down progress and generally strains the working relationship among the participants. Escalations should be exceptions. There are ways to discourage it. In larger organizations, you can, for example, require that the vice presidents of the teams involved in the disagreement escalate the issue. Most of the time the vice president has a high enough purview to remove the need for the escalation at all. Sometimes managing disagreements requires managing personalities. You can find many books on working with difficult personalities at any bookstore.

Rationale

> 6. Do you share the rationale for your decisions with your employees?

Tell employees why you are doing what you do.

This is a simple and obvious concept but it is overlooked at times. If you take the time to tell people why you are doing something, they are a lot more likely to help you be successful than if you do not. You should also enlist them to provide you with better solutions. Enlisting their good ideas implies that you have to talk to them early enough to have those ideas make a difference.

One example is where I was consulting for a company that had a software only product and the executives wanted to move to an appliance based product. The engineering team's expertise was not in the area of systems or appliances and they were both afraid of and skeptical about the change. The reason the company wanted to change to the appliance model was because the software only solution required too much work for customers to deploy the product. By spending time explaining this to engineering, I was able to quell their fears and get support for the new plan.

Another example was at Sun Microsystems when we were moving Solaris to a quarterly release model; one senior engineer said that quarterly releases were "evil". I was having a senior engineer meeting and the quarterly release was one of the main topics. I presented my rationale and the engineer persisted. I asked him what he would do instead to deal with the requirements and he said he did not know. He never backed down from his position but agreed to disagree, and the vehemence of rhetoric diminished greatly.

If I had not spent the time to have the discussion, there would be ongoing unaddressed dissatisfaction that could grow into wider unrest. Instead, I felt that my relationships with developers grew because of taking the time and effort to explain rationale. We learned more about each other. We trusted each other more. It engendered loyalty.

Venues

> 7. Have you established regular meetings with different constituencies in your organization?

It takes different venues to reach engineers. Sometimes they need to hear something more than once. Sometimes they need to be in an environment with which they are comfortable to really absorb information or be willing to question it.

The following are the kinds of meetings that you should have regularly:

- All hands meetings
    - This means everyone! Include temps, interns, secretaries, etc. (minimum once per quarter).
- One-on-one meetings
    - You should meet with your direct reports on a biweekly basis for at least one half hour.

- Group meetings
    - Meet with your direct reports weekly as a group.
- Skip-level meetings
    - Meet with individuals and groups one or more levels down in your organization once or twice a year with and without their managers.
- Site meetings
    - Meet with a whole site on a regular basis (minimum once per quarter).
- Senior engineer meetings
    - These are the influencers and thought leaders. Get them to help define and drive your agenda. Have these three or four times per year.
- Team building meetings.
    - Take the time to do organizational development. The act of stopping your day-to-day activities and focusing on an area for improvement will have a positive impact. Try to do this at least a couple of times per year.
- Social meetings
    - It is useful to know the people you are dealing with on a human level. Run these a minimum of once per quarter.
- Manager meetings
    - Meet with all managers once a month.
- Impromptu meetings
    - Walk the halls on an ongoing basis and make opportunities to talk to people.

The content for each of these meetings will vary. They should be used to drive the elevator pitch (see the *Elevator Pitch* section) for your organization, but there are unique needs for each group. You should listen to their ideas and issues. You should not direct anyone in those meetings who does not report to you directly – remember to work through their managers. If you direct people who are not direct reports, it disempowers their managers and constitutes micromanagement. Furthermore, if your direction conflicts with their manager's direction, your developers may get confused about what they should be doing.

Remember that different cultures communicate in different venues as well. Some may not interact in an official group work situation but open up over dinner. Take the time to figure out how to best reach your folks and how they feel comfortable reaching you.

> **8. Do you have a communication plan?**

Sit down with your staff and write down what meetings, email communications, status rollups, etc. you will have. Make the list and publish it. Find out whether your team is accomplishing the goals in the communication plan periodically and make adjustments where necessary.

Consensus

> **9. Do you take the time to bring key stakeholders into the decision process?**

It is my firm belief that you cannot run most engineering organizations as democracies and efficiently accomplish your goals. However, it is important to take the time to get buy-in and some degree of consensus. The more buy-in you have, the more motivated and loyal your team will be.

Consensus is not reached in a group forum.

Full consensus is hard to achieve period. Along the road to consensus you should reach a quorum and that is really what this section is about.

When you want to make changes in an organization, it is imperative to have a plan. This plan could include written role-out plans, key employee discussions, group meetings, etc. Just take some time and think about what you are doing.

Consensus is achieved with individuals not groups. You must talk to individuals in one-on-one situations. You must find the key influencers and stakeholders and talk to them. If they are informed and understand your rationale, they will be able to have a reasonable conversation with others about it and provide support for your plans in group meetings. This has to do with "No surprises" and respect.

Even if you do not reach full consensus, the process described above is important because it engenders discussion and understanding.

> 10. Do you develop communication plans when you are rolling out big announcements or changes?

Organizational change is a time when a well thought out communication plan is critical. Even though you may decide how to make changes in a small group, once the decisions are in place do what is described above. Put together a plan:

- Written announcement review
- Discussions with key stakeholders (people who are heavily affected and people who are influential in the organization)
- Group meeting
- General announcement
- One week follow up
- One month follow up
- Plan approval by management and human resources

Taking the time to think about this will make it easier to implement changes and get buy-in.

Messages and Rules

> 11. Do you communicate goals and consequences along with rules?

You have two tools to effect change in an organization: messages and rules.

It doesn't make a difference if it is something small like participating in planning vacations so everyone is not gone at once from the office or something bigger like changing the relationship between your group and some other group – you have the same two tools.

It is important that you use both judiciously. Rules are bureaucracy. Few developers like bureaucracy. If you make too many rules or institute them too quickly, you are likely to have a revolt. However, this is the big difference between managing in the small versus managing in the large. You cannot just handle issues in an ad hoc fashion as your organization grows. Recognizing this difference is one of the skills I look for in a second line manager as they think about becoming a third line manager.

One metaphor I like to use when talking about messages and rules is that of taking a trip. It is usually easier to motivate the passengers and driver if they know what the end destination is. If all they have are directions, they could get anxious, impatient, and unhappy.

Messages are destinations. If you don't tell your team where you want to head, it is hard for them to follow. Do not assume they can deduce the destination from the directions. It is also important that you provide directions or rules for them to follow. You need to pick these carefully and make sure they make sense. Too many destinations (or directions for that matter) will just confuse your team.

You need to bind rules back to the messages, and you need to hold people accountable. Do not make rules unless you are willing to follow through with consequences.

Here are some examples:

Message:

> "Employees are important to this company and we will make sure that we complete a useful yearly review for each employee on time."

Rules:

> "Managers must complete training for doing useful reviews before they start the review process."
>
> "Managers must complete their employee's reviews in advance of their own review being completed." (This allows the consequence below to be implemented.)
>
> "Employees must provide input to the review by a prescribed date."

Consequences:

> "Managers and employees who do not follow the review rules will have adverse consequences in their own reviews."

Message:

"Employees in this group must maintain respect for other groups."

Rules:

"Flame email will not be tolerated."

"Abusive confrontations in meetings will not be tolerated."

"Uncooperative behavior will not be tolerated."

Consequences:

"Depending on the severity of the action, all or part of the following consequences will be implemented:

- Apology required
- Performance plan put in place
- Termination"

Message:

> "We are integrating open-source technology into our product and plan to be open-source compatible."

Rules

> "Funding will reflect adequate resources to accomplish the work."
>
> "Plans will be drawn up to specify, develop, and release products that reflect the message."
>
> "Everyone has to help as appropriate."

Consequences

> "Those who hinder this effort will be put under a performance plan."
>
> "The group will be measured by the success of the plan and execution."

In all these cases, management must follow through. If you send messages and make rules and you don't follow through, your messages and rules will become less potent.

As I indicated above, in smaller groups this whole process may be ad hoc and you might not realize when you are messaging and when you are making a rule. It is important that you recognize the difference as you manage larger organizations (when you have managers reporting to you) because you can confuse your reports about what you are standing firm on (a rule) and in what direction you want the team to head (a message).

Be careful about your words. You can use them premeditatedly and inspire or focus a group. You can also cause damage by not paying attention.

Some final words here: it bears repeating that engineers bridle at bureaucracy. Try to be sparing with rules.

Managing Up

> 12. Do you take the time to communicate with upper management?

Many people forget to communicate to their manager, their manager's manager, and their manager's peers.

It is important to understand that you need to influence other people in the executive team besides your boss. If your boss is the only one arguing for your team's budgets or rewards at meetings with your manager's peers, your manager will have a very hard task. If you spend time influencing other executives, they will help your team and your career.

Develop a direct working relationship with your manager's manager. Having that relationship can help you and your team during budgeting and reviews as well as during periods of organizational chaos or change.

Another important thing to keep in mind is to align yourself with the way in which your company makes money. The groups that bring in the most revenue will often have the most influence. It is your duty as a good employee and manager to determine how you can help that group or effort. It will also mean more recognition and opportunities for your team.

Spend time to make sure your team's goals match what your manger thinks your team's goals should be. Resolve disconnects. Nothing could be worse than surprising your manager or being in conflict with your manager on key issues.

Finally, remember that your manager and other executives worked hard to get to where they are. They are in responsible positions and deserve your respect. Honor them and they are more likely to honor you.

Chapter 2: Roles and Responsibilities

Over the years, I have developed a lot of beliefs on how to run successful organizations. Like most things, you have to start from the beginning and the beginning really is: "What does everyone do?" Without that being clear, it is hard to accomplish anything and it is easy to have disagreements.

This chapter starts out with a cardinal rule, *One Owner*. After that we spend some time on organizational structure with sections on *Matrix Management, Steering, Program Management,* and *Quality Assurance*. Then we talk about some attributes that help define and measure roles with sections on *Information vs. Decisions*, *Delegation, Accountability,* and *Identifying Roles*. Finally, I talk a bit about your role as a manager in a section entitled *Separation*.

One Owner

> 13. *Have you identified one and only one owner for projects, products, tasks, etc?*

Instituting a rule that requires identifying one owner will allow your organization to achieve results and accountability.

The number one way to ensure that you don't get a job done is to assign it to two people. There are lots of variations on this problem where roles are ambiguous or the person owning the problem has no authority. It does not matter if you are talking about a small action item or the success of a 500-person organization; there has to be one owner.

I always hearken back to a comment as to why people used integrators to deploy solutions – they would say they wanted "one throat to choke". If someone knows his or her job or business is on the line for delivering, they are more likely to deliver.

There had been big transitions in our product management department at a company where I was working; and we had various people in charge, some in temporary positions, temporarily in charge, etc. In the vacuum, the company had to move forward. The relationship between engineering and product management deteriorated somewhat.

We had a meeting to discuss a number of issues causing friction. I told the vice president of marketing that one of the issues was that my managers complained that they were not in the loop. I also told him that my team felt that some of the product managers had been trying to dictate implementation and schedule of the product, and my managers were unhappy about it. The vice president of marketing thought it was all right for product management to be involved in implementations discussions. I agreed but said that it had to be driven by engineering and not product management.

The vice president of marketing went on to describe an instance where product management got disparate estimates from engineers than those from the engineering manager. The engineering manager admonished the engineers for supplying information that conflicted with the information that he had provided. Product management also felt its access to engineers was being restricted.

I asked if anyone escalated to me and the answer was no.

This is a good example of where it is imperative to define roles and responsibilities. In this case I would observe the following:

- It is product management's job to drive requirements, collateral, priorities, etc. It is product management's job to define which person in their organization drives these jobs.
- It is engineering's job to drive architecture, implementation, estimate, etc. It is engineering's job to define which person in their organization drives these jobs.
- Everyone should be allowed access to any meeting deciding about product related items regardless of who drives.
- If there is an issue that is either too sensitive (like a lack of trust of estimates) or cannot be resolved, it should be escalated up the management chain after two attempts to resolve conflict.

It is everyone's job to bring to the attention of management items that are not being attended to.

By clearly articulating these roles, it would become obvious who is responsible for what. Engineering won't be putting up walls. If engineering says scheduling is the job of an engineering manager, then product management must work through them to get schedules. If they don't like the schedules and cannot get resolution from the responsible party, they need to escalate.

In the above example, none of this happened. Instead both sides got angry at each other, trust disintegrated, and progress did not happen at the desired pace.

Don't leave a meeting without assigning owners to action items along with dates for the item to get resolved.

Don't create organizations where it is ambiguous as to who owns architecture, projects, technology, resources, etc.

Make sure all communications regarding an owner either flows through the owner or includes the owner. If the owner is the true source of information about their area, it helps avoid he-said, she-said situations.

Hold the people who are owners accountable. If you do not, then ownership will mean nothing and other people will try to step in and solve the problem and the same bad behaviors will occur.

Matrix Organizations

> 14. Have you identified cross-functional organizations and reporting structures?

All successful organizations have learned how to matrix manage.

Matrix management refers to a method of management where a person or group has some amount of reporting structure to multiple managers. Usually those managers represent different goals or projects or products.

One big discussion that is repeated over and over again is how to organize a software group. Do you organize by projects or by functional areas? Either way you organize, you have to matrix manage.

I know that there are variations in terms around the industry so I will start this section by defining what I mean by a project versus functional organization. I will then go on to describe advantages and disadvantages with each and which I favor.

A project may be a release or subcomponent of a release. Let's say you are developing an email program. In a very pure project organization, all of the people working on that project would report up to the same manager. The developers would not be working on anything else. The manager would have no other responsibilities but this release. This would include:

- Protocol developers (IMAP, POP3, SMTP, etc.)
- Data Store developers (filing and managing messages)
- Application developers (GUI)
- QA developers
- QA testers
- Release engineers
- Documentation engineers

The manager would not have to go to anyone to get resources to get the project done.

In contrast, in a pure functional organization, each of the groups listed above would be part of a team that worked on similar technologies in many projects or releases.

For example, the Protocol developers might also work on an LDAP or DNS protocol for another product. Or the protocol developers might be working on tasks for multiple releases – either fixing bugs for previous releases or working on long lead-time projects for future releases.

In most organizations, there are hybrids. Some developers might be dedicated under a single manager for a particular project and some may be shared (e.g. QA, Documentation, etc.).

If you organize by project and you have more than one project, you have to coordinate between functional areas if you want to have consistency and code reuse between projects. For example, you will probably want to share one test framework for all of your projects. This requires coordination.

You will also probably want some amount of discussion occurring between your protocol people working on different projects so that you share drivers or network stacks between those projects. This requires coordination.

You may have a mixed environment as discussed above and have some shared resources like documentation writers. This takes coordination.

Someone should have the responsibility of coordinating cross project activities for each shared area. These will be matrix managers or project leads.

> 15. Have you developed mechanisms to authorize people running cross-functional organizations to succeed?

If you organize by function, you will need to coordinate to get projects done. Without assigning someone to drive a project, no one will be responsible for cross-functional integration, schedule dependencies, etc. Without an owner, a release will not happen. Clearly, the coordination between functional areas becomes a larger task than in a project organization in order to ensure coherency within the project.

The advantage of project organizations is that you can direct the people on your project. While this may provide a warm and fuzzy feeling, in reality it is rarely the case that you fully control the people on your project. People get sidetracked in either type of organization, and it takes leadership to insure that projects get the right amount of attention.

The advantage of a functional organization is that there is a greater chance for communication between people working on like things. It is easier to get consistency in a particular area and it is easier for folks to influence projects and see a career path in their area of expertise. It is also easier to have a technical manager who is expert in a particular area be successful with a functional team than with a diverse team with different skill sets and work styles (quality assurance, documentation, networking, operation systems, tools, etc.).

The downside of functional organizations is that it is harder to get projects out. It is easier to reallocate resources for emergencies or other projects. It takes leadership to ensure that resources are not diverted.

In very small organizations, there may very well be only one project, and there is no difference between the two kinds of organization in that environment. As organizations and the tasks they take on grow, the organization will face these issues on how to organize.

I prefer the functional organizations because, as mentioned above, I have found that the long term productivity and happiness of employees is greater, and because you have to matrix-manage either way.

Steering

> 16. Have you established cross-functional teams to define and drive your products and projects?

It is important to define and drive your products in a premeditated way.

In many companies, committees help define and drive products. This is important because it is critical that you take a holistic view of a product in order to ensure success. The components include:

- Product definition
- Competitive positioning
- Training

- Rollout
- Upgrade
- Support
- Specifications
- End of life

The committee should at least have the following representation:

- Product Management
- Support
- Engineering Management
- Engineering Technologist
- Sales

Very clearly, in small companies one person may represent multiple constituencies. These representatives, however, must be authorized to make decisions. You cannot afford second-guessing.

One person must run the committee and be responsible for its success (see the section on *One Owner*). The committee should be responsible for:

- Adopting and developing processes
- Defining product (see the sections on *Strategy* and *Criteria*)
- Status and accountability

If you have multiple products, you need an overview committee that approves the projects and products across the multiple subcommittees to ensure consistency across the company, minimizing redundancy, and maximizing company sales across the products. In small companies it may be the same committee driving multiple products and ensuring consistency between them.

Program Management

> 17. Do you have program managers and have you identified their responsibilities?

Program management is critical to successfully releasing any product.

This goes directly to roles and responsibilities. While a director, vice president, or manager may be responsible for developing or releasing a product, they have other day-to-day chores. These usually include people management, hiring, budgets, product definition, customer interaction, firefighting, etc. If no single person is responsible for driving and coordinating the schedules and deliverables for a product, the product will not release in a timely fashion.

There are different kinds of program managers. Some have specific names in organizations, but they all manage programs. It is important to recognize the different tasks they do and the different skills required for those tasks. The jobs include:

- Developing, collecting, coalescing, and maintaining schedules
- Tracking deliverables
- Managing committees
- Quality measurements
- Liaison between groups within a company
- Liaison with vendors and/or customers outside the company

The scope of their work may vary greatly as well. Some may be assigned to a small group and others to larger groups. One may have an impulse to lump these jobs together and it is rare that someone can be competent in all of them.

I have been in some organizations that have wholly discounted program management. There are many causes for this and I have listed some in the following paragraphs.

One reason some organizations discount program management is that we often assign roles to program managers who do not have the technical competence to do the job. If they are just a document coalescer, as opposed to a content coalescer, then it is hard to differentiate between program managers and administrators. In fact many administrators go into program management as a mechanism to grow their careers. When they present their data and they cannot speak to content, it is easy for people to lose confidence in their value.

Another reason that program managers have a tough road is the nature of their job. They are supposed to keep things moving and raise the flag as things go wrong and do all this without the authority to manage the resources. Some companies like IBM and Microsoft have powerful program managers that control budgets and therefore have more authority, but they still have to matrix-manage. Many program managers are tough and dogmatic and this makes them unpopular in organizations.

During economically challenging times, I have had pressure to reduce or remove them from my organizations; but I would not give in on this. I can be more than twice as productive with a good program manager as I can work on my own as a manager.

The best program managers I have worked with have the following qualities:

- They have a service mentality where the customer is right no matter what.
- They cajole and move things forward unobtrusively.
- They know when to let their managers handle unmovable situations.
- They are technical enough to tell when they need more information. They should be able to detect people sandbagging on schedules or things that just don't seem consistent.
- They are technical enough to make presentations.
- They communicate well.
- They consolidate well.
- They can determine when they need help.

I would not want to run any organization without program managers.

Quality Assurance

> 18. Have you established how your organization will do quality assurance and who is responsible for it?

Quality is everyone's responsibility.

The most frequent question I am asked is how to organize software quality assurance organizations:

- Should it be a separate organization?
- Should quality engineers be part of the reporting structure of a development team?
- How do you handle automation versus test development versus test execution?
- What should the ratio be between developers and the quality team?

It seems to me that these questions are tactical, and I will address them later; but the first questions have to do with attitude and goals. Who is responsible for quality and how do you know you have it?

The first thing I tell people is that I hold the product development managers responsible for the quality of the product. They cannot point fingers saying some quality organization did not do their job. Once you make it clear who is responsible, the decision of where it goes is somewhat academic. Quality engineers are a crucial part of the team, but they are part of the team.

The second thing I tell people is to agree upon what is important. See the section on *Criteria*. If you do not know what you are measuring, you cannot determine whether you are making your quality goals. If you define your goals in detail, it also removes any question about integrity.

Some people assume that development engineers do not respect quality and that having the quality organizations within engineering is like having a fox watching the henhouse. If you know what the goals are and you do not release until you meet those goals, this becomes a non-issue. Using criteria makes it an objective process to decide when to stop a release because of quality issues and does not put the quality team in the position of being the bad cop.

Now to address some tactical issues:

- You need someone who believes it is their day job to run a QA team. If you can get your development manager to do that, it would be great; but many times it is not their area of interest and expertise (see the section on *Matrix Organizations*).
- Automation is the key. If you cannot get your QA automated, you will not be able to produce products and patches in a timely fashion.
- A ratio of developers to quality assurance developers or testers does not matter. Take a look at the work you need to do and schedule it. Try using contractors initially before you commit to fulltime personnel.
- Don't underestimate the execution piece. Do not make developers do ongoing test execution as part of their jobs. It is poor cost/benefit tradeoff and they will get bored.

Information vs. Decisions

> 19. Do you achieve the balance in your organizations to both allow a free flow of information and identify the owners of decisions?

Make decisions in a hierarchical fashion, but do not impose hierarchies on information (dissemination, discussions, etc.).

It is easy to let you or your teams fail to communicate. You can justify it saying that information is not complete and that you have to get closure before sharing. This will not promote trust between your organization and other organizations. In order to promote trust within your organization, sharing of information should be like voting in Chicago: early and often.

Do not confuse this with ownership. While it is important to drive and push information out, the person responsible for the project should make the decisions about the areas for which you have empowered them. If you do not make it clear who owns a decision and that there is a difference between discussions and decisions, confusion will ensue. Developers will think they get direction from multiple people and be unhappy, and you will not reach your goals.

The relationship between engineering and product management at one of the companies where I worked (the same company I discussed above) was a great example of where the difference between information sharing and decision-making were not clear. Product management had been pretty dysfunctional and engineering had to pick up some of the work. Changes were made in product management personnel. The new product management personnel were more competent but not great at relationship building. Engineering became protectionist and defensive. Product management drove harder and became bitter, and engineering bridled at product management trying to do their job.

In the end, product management felt that engineering was too isolationist and hierarchical. Engineering felt that product management didn't respect their ownership of implementation and design. The great news is that we had hired a new vice president of marketing, and he and I had some frank conversations. We got some help from the CEO and CTO and got clear on what we needed to do. We sent a strong message to the combined team that there were no boundaries in communication, but there were still clear roles and responsibilities.

Delegation

> 20. Have you established what decisions you are willing to delegate and what decisions need to be finalized through you?

You cannot do it alone!

From the time you are in first grade, you are asked to excel as an individual. You are asked to do your own homework and complete your tests by yourself. While some schools and classes concentrate on helping people learn skills to rely on others, it is not commonplace.

There is also a fine line with regard to trust. I have seen many Vice Presidents not deliver their products on time because they delegated everything and were too trusting. See the section on *Accountability* that addresses this.

So what should you delegate? Everything you can.

You cannot delegate until you know what the requirements are. If you are delegating the collection of requirements, then you better check them before you let the project proceed. The way you enable the feeling of empowerment is not to second-guess and not to implement for someone. The only way to get what you want is to specify your requirements and make sure the people to whom you delegate are accountable for those requirements.

When you review the status or results of the project, try to limit your comments to the requirements you set forth. If you forgot a requirement, acknowledge that and take some blame. Clearly there are some requirements that are common sense but err on the side of it being your fault.

See the section on *Identifying Roles*. Help your people succeed.

Accountability

> 21. Have you developed mechanisms to determine when people and teams are off course?

Don't confuse micromanagement and accountability.

See the section on *Delegation*. Now that you have delegated, how are you going to ensure that your organization accomplishes the tasks at hand? Accountability is critical to the health and success of any organization. Both your company's success and your personal career depend upon it.

Execution is king and I have seen many people in management lose interest in day-to-day operations as their careers grow. Strategy or customer interactions attract them and they neglect execution. This is, at the risk of repeating myself, a great recipe for failure. If you have reached a point where you are more attracted by other things, get out of direct line management.

Most engineers grow in their careers by doing things on their own. There are still many organizations that do not require things like design and code reviews. I know that many engineers look at reviews, consciously or unconsciously, as an affront or lack of trust in their work. But reviews are just good hygiene and the only way to get quality products.

The same principles are true for schedules and plans. Those same engineers became managers and many managers looked at reviews as an affront. They do not want to report status or have their plans scrutinized. It is easy for managers to feel they are being micromanaged if they are held accountable or asked to share information. They will only learn over time that it is not.

Your staff needs to experience the feeling of being empowered where they are expected to drive a project plan and still have reviews. They need to feel they are not second-guessed all the time. This is tricky because any comment you make on a plan can be construed as second-guessing.

Make sure that your team, managers, or developers are involved in the development of plans and schedules. It is hard for people to feel accountable for a schedule if they did not buy in to the schedule. See the section on *Schedules*.

Make clear what you are doing and spend time listening to people. See the section on *Make Them Feel Heard*.

Identifying Roles

> 22. Have you identified the roles in your organization and who is responsible for those roles?

Take the time to identify roles.

You can choose to do this when you start a project or build the group, but you have to have a discussion about what kind of roles are necessary and who will fill those roles. When teams change or grow, employees' roles change. Acknowledge this and bring the team together to help define roles.

Define the following:
- The role.
- The owner.
- The constituents that need to help the owner accomplish their task.
- The escalation path in case people do not like some decision that the owner has made.

Defining roles is about empowerment and boundaries. Without these definitions it is ambiguous as to who does what.

Here are some of the roles that you might consider identifying owners for:

- Product engineering
- Product definition
- Development process definition
- Release process definition
- People management
- Schedules
- Technical leadership
- Quality assessment
- Test development
- Lab infrastructure
- Training

Some of these items may be matrixed and broken down into one or more groups. For example technical leadership might actually be

- Release leads
- Technology leads
- Component leads

The release and technology leads have overlapping leadership responsibilities in their areas of ownership. An example of this overlap is that the technology leadership may be in networking, and component leadership might be in networking security and mobile networking. The point here is to realize that someone must oversee all of the networking components to make sure they work in synch across releases. The release lead has to make sure that multiple components and technologies work in synch for a particular release.

One example of a role might be product engineering. The owner of product engineering might be responsible for building final releases, testing the release to make sure it is installable, getting approval from the contributors for each release and delivering the release to support so they can provide it to customers. The owner might be an engineering manager. The contributors would be the product team including support, product management, and engineering; and the escalation path would be to the vice president of engineering.

Another example would be technical leadership for a product. The technical lead would be a senior developer or architect. The contributors would be the engineers on the project, other senior engineers in the company, product management, and support. The technical lead would be responsible for making sure all technical decisions get made and technical issues are resolved. They would also be responsible for making sure the product is consistent across technical disciplines and for supporting the creation, monitoring and adjusting of schedules.

Remember pick one owner for each role. Your list of roles or jobs will differ from company to company and will change over time. Don't change too often.

See the *Project Example Appendix* for a detailed example.

Separation

> 23. Do you and your managers behave in a way that differentiates them from developers?

It is important to realize that you are not one of the troops.

I had a boss who said being a manager means eating alone. It was a metaphor to say that you really are separate. If you try to be a pal or one of the gang, it will not work. The folks who are working for you need to know you are their boss.

It is important that you stick to your role; otherwise it gets confusing. Developers interact with other developers differently than they do with their boss. If you are the boss and you are in a design meeting speaking your mind on implementation details, your developers may take it as a directive instead of a discussion. Your developers will not use their creativity and they can become resentful and think you are micromanaging. You want your employees to feel comfortable disagreeing in a positive and constructive manner.

If you are very technical, one of the tricks you can use to try to ensure that you are not dictating implementation is to try and state everything as requirements. From that position you can more easily question your team. For example, dictate the requirement that code must be maintainable, and newcomers must be capable of picking up the code and working on it or dictate that there must be some development conventions. After dictating these requirements, delegate developing those conventions to senior engineers. If it comes back missing something, ask how it meets the requirements and do not ask why they are not doing it some other way.

24. Do you and your managers respect the privacy of their employees?

Another aspect of this has to do with privacy. As a developer you might gossip in the hall. As a manager you must protect people's personal or job related information. One of the first mistakes I made as a manager was regarding this issue. I had been a project leader of a few people and had just been made manager. One of the developers had been dating someone in the company and had kept a tight lid on it. Almost no one knew. We knew he was seeing someone but not who. He went away on vacation and while he was gone, I guessed and told someone else and it spread. After that I lost his trust. It would not have been as bad a thing (although still not right) as a fellow developer, but it was unacceptable as a manager.

Take this issue seriously.

We are now in an interesting period of time where the government and the public are scrutinizing company executives. Events at Worldcom and Enron pointed out the ill effects resulting from the behavior of management. You do not have to do something illegal to ruin a company. Your behavior both inside the company walls and outside them can affect morale and company success. Separation here means holding yourself to a higher standard. Be responsible and behave responsibly.

Chapter 3: Strategy

There are many books that provide a lot of information on how to develop strategy. This chapter does none of that. It discusses the mechanics and processes around strategy as well as some of the psychology related to it. The section titled *Engineer's Lament* speaks about the importance of having strategies for your organization, the *Elevator Pitch section* discusses the importance of getting everyone on the same page, and the section entitled *Context and Organization* details some mechanisms you can use to organize and have meaningful strategies.

Engineer's Lament

> **25. Do you and your team believe the strategy?**

A common engineer lament is, "This Company has no direction. I do not know how what I do has any relevance to company success."

Engineers may not always vocalize the above sentiment in quite the way I have stated it, but it is very common. It is important to develop a strategy on which to base funding and resource decisions, but it is also important to give your team a sense of purpose and a framework within which to make day-to-day technical decisions.

When I originally joined the Solaris team at Sun we had about 2000 engineers from all around Sun who contributed to the product. Each project they worked on went to a central committee for approval. Proposals came in all forms from a one-page email to 30 page elaborate presentations. The committee couldn't tell whether a project was consistent with other projects and whether they would help the company to be more successful. As a result people worked on projects that didn't fit together or projects the customers never used, and we didn't produce overall solutions that could be marketed and sold easily.

Consistency, context and central control issues all contributed to our engineers concerns. In order to help address those issues, we worked on three things:

- Requiring that projects fit into well defined strategies
- Normalizing the proposal format
- Developing a committee hierarchy to distribute responsibility

Elevator Pitch

> **26. Does your company have a strategy that is easy to articulate?**

Sometimes it is hard to see the forest for the trees.

It does not matter whether you are talking about a small organization or a large one; it is easy to get caught up in details and individual projects and not remember what the destination is. It is a lot easier to have a discussion about whether to do a project, spend money, or go after a customer if you know where you want to be. Sometimes you might take a tangent, but do so in a premeditated way. Do not end up off course for long.

Clearly, in big organizations there may be a hierarchy of elevator pitches but there has to be one -- a paradigm by which to measure everything.

In Solaris, my elevator pitch was that if you ran an application on Solaris in three to five years, "it just worked". It shouldn't matter what resources it required, what disk space or users needed to be provisioned; you would tell Solaris what you needed and it would ensure your application would run. Clearly you need good infrastructure to reach this goal but there are features in Solaris 10 that speak directly to this: most notably containers and fault management.

This gave a rallying point and a way to measure what we did.

At Infoblox, my elevator pitch was to manage your data and not protocols. A lot of people use RADIUS, LDAP and DNS without understanding the protocols. They get overwhelmed with the arcane nature of their protocols. They have high overhead in the operational costs of managing them. The elevator pitch resonates because all they want to do is manage users, hosts, and IP addresses. They do not want to worry about primary this or time to live that. All of the work we were doing was toward that principle.

Context and Organization

> 27. Do you have processes that allow your strategy to both scale and remain consistent within your company?

It turned out that at any one time, people around Sun were working on about 300 projects that they wanted to deliver into Solaris. We took a look at these and realized that there was no context with which to make a decision about whether the project was good. Therefore, the committee turned into a rubber stamp committee. We did some hard work and developed 17 strategies that embodied the different feature areas for Solaris. Some were vertical strategies representing discrete technologies like networking or data management and others were more horizontal like reliability or performance.

Since mapping 17 strategies to 300 projects does not translate easily, we introduced the concept of sub-strategies or what we called programs. If networking was a strategy, wireless was a program under the networking strategy, and mobile IP was a project under the wireless program.

We also noticed that various programs and projects fit under multiple strategies or programs. For example, networking performance was a program under the networking strategy and the performance strategy. This enabled our teams to make sure our investment in networking performance was consistent within the networking strategy (easy) and within all of the performance projects across technologies like data management and memory management (harder).

> 28. Can you and your team articulate the strategy?

You should figure out the correct level of granularity for your company. Small companies will not need multiple levels of strategies. Make sure everyone in your group can articulate the high level strategy and the sub-strategies that apply to it.

Once you agree on a strategy, do not approve projects that do not fit into the strategies without premeditation. This will be the forcing function that makes your strategies a reality. Without project approval, there should be no way to proceed with a project.

This is a very exciting mechanism because not only do you get to make decisions in context, you also have a chance to ensure your team develops high-level strategies for the product. These processes will allow you to see the forest for the trees and begin to execute on bigger, more strategic projects.

> 29. Have you developed templates that provide disparate projects and products a way to present the data for their strategies in common terms agreed to by your company?

Part of the process of driving an organization to change requires finding a common language to talk about strategies. Many organizational programs such as Six Sigma™ (see the section on *Continuous Improvement* for more discussion about such programs) encourage similar things. Here is an outline for a sample 7 slide strategy presentation you can use:

- Overview
- Taxonomy
    - What things are important to describe/measure how we are doing for this strategy? For example, in networking it might be performance, standards, interoperability, field training, etc.
- Competitive Report Card
    - This grades your product today, your product tomorrow, how it compares with competitors, etc. against the taxonomy using A, B, C or filled in circle kind of grades.
- Today's Picture
    - A literal picture showing what we have today.

- Tomorrow's Picture
    - A literal picture of where we want to be tomorrow.
- Projects/Programs Required
- Resources Required

Spend time reviewing these slides with the presenter before they go to the committee. It makes a huge difference.

The hardest part is the pictures. By forcing teams to develop a visual representation of where they are and where they want to be, you force them to think about the big picture.

One example here would be the networking strategy at Sun. Solaris 10 provides a new network stack that allows specific consumers to bypass generic networking stack code. They provide a framework to enhance performance when you know what the networking traffic is and who the consumer of the networking traffic is (e.g. http and webservers). The original today picture showed the onerous task of packets working their way through the old networking stack along with an increasing number of well-known protocols and consumers. The tomorrow picture showed those consumers cutting a swath through the stack with a faster path. The picture presented a simple concept and was very effective in communicating the proposed changes.

A sample strategy proposal is presented in the *Project Example Appendix*.

You can use the same format for strategy and programs and a similar one for projects. Here is one possible format for a project proposal:

- Overview (including which strategy it fits into)
- Business Case
- Feature list
    - High-level list of what the customer will see
    - Include a list of what is not included but might be expected

- Quality
    - Are there new tests that need to be written?
    - What tests must it pass?
    - Are there new criteria for the product because of this project?
- Resources
    - Are people and equipment already allocated and on-board?
- Schedules
    - What are the major milestones and dates?
    - Is there a detailed schedule?
- Issues/Challenges

A project proposal sample is presented in the *Project Example Appendix*.

You can consider each slide of both the strategy and project presentations to be a boundary for the strategy, program, or project. Approval would be required if a change were needed.

Make sure that the presentations use the right granularity for their boundaries. For example, if a project presentation says it will deliver on March 15th and it misses that date by one day, it would need approval again by the same committee that approved the project. Ask yourself if that is really what you want. Most of the time if a product delivers within a month or a quarter, that will still meet the company's goals. Providing this leeway also empowers the team to make small changes without a huge re-approval process.

Require a product management and an engineering representative to jointly present the proposal with input from other constituencies. Pick the people who will drive the implementation to develop and present the strategy, program, or project.

In a large organization, strategies and programs should be approved by a top-level steering committee (see the section on *Steering*). Developing the strategies and programs becomes the purview of subcommittees chartered by the top-level committee. The subcommittees are also responsible for approving projects.

Architectural committees dealing with technical designs and interfaces would be asked only to approve an architecture proposal that was part of an approved project. By closing the loop, it helps ensure that the company has well defined strategies and that projects are consistent with those strategies.

So this seems like a lot of bureaucracy. Does it work? Is the strategy process worth it? I think so. At Sun, this process was like planting seeds, and most of the results can be seen in Solaris 9 and Solaris 10. The Solaris groups had been accused of being incremental bug fixers; this process not only provided a more coherent product to sell but helped kick-start innovation in a group that had been held back since the SunOS™ days. Sun has great engineers, but they needed a chance to innovate; this enabled them to do so.

I remember having a discussion with an engineer who was responsible for helping design the RAS (Reliability, Availability, and Serviceability) strategy. He said. "If I spend time on this, all these bugs won't get fixed." I told him that if he decided not to work on strategy, all he would ever get to do is fix bugs, and eventually the company would go out of business. I do not know if Solaris 10 will keep Sun in business, but I am certain it is essential for Sun's success.

30. Do you have processes in place to map the strategy to a roadmap?

It is clear that you need to bind strategies back to budgets. I will talk about that in the section on *Budgets*.

Your organization may not be as big as Sun's, but the same principles apply in smaller doses. Decide on your strategies and what it will take to accomplish them.

Chapter 4: Resources

When you become a software developer or a manager, no one teaches you how to run a business. It is important to be the kind of person who could make trade-offs and know how much money is available at all times. This chapter has some of the basics on what you need to create and run *Budgets* for your organization and manage human resources with the *Hiring* and *Layoff* sections.

Budgets

> 31. Do you have a well-defined budget process?

Budgets should be your highest priority task.

Without budgets, you cannot hire people or purchase equipment or accomplish anything. This is a cart-before-the-horse thing. Make this your team's highest priority.

When I started to learn programming in school, there were great discussions about which method of programming was correct: top-down or bottom-up. I learned over time, as most others did, that you had to do both simultaneously. If you just did top down, you would miss fundamental implementation issues that could cause great rework; and if you just did bottom-up, it got hard to have global organization, planning, and re-use. Budgeting is exactly the same as programming. You must do both top-down and bottom-up budgeting at the same time.

I learned the best top down budgeting technique from Clark Masters at Sun. He was responsible for Sun's high-end servers. While Sun sold a lot of machines into the enterprise market, he was also the executive who owned High Performance Computing (HPC) for the company. I asked him how he decided how much to invest in HPC since it was a relatively small part of his revenue stream. He told me he manipulated the investment level in categories like high-level knobs. He listed the areas that were important to him and he guessed at a high level how much he wanted to invest (30% on one category, 20% on another, etc.). He just pegged the HPC investment at 10% even though it was not bringing in 10% of his revenues. He did this because he was responsible for making HPC a success.

The categories become a taxonomy of what the values are to your customer.

Take this to heart and do the same thing. Group your investments into a small number of categories and take an inventory of how much you are investing in each and adjust based on high-level goals. When I was working at Sun, the categories for Solaris were:

- Reliability/Availability/Serviceability (RAS)
- Performance/Scalability
- Standards
- Security
- Management
- Productization

The company had a growing emphasis on RAS, but our investment there was low so I bumped it up.

These categories also give you a way to talk to employees and customers about what you are doing. It makes an effective and comprehensive story to say here are all the projects we are doing to enhance performance or security.

32. Do you have a list of what each person is working on?

The bottom up part is an interesting exercise as well. The first thing you have to do is find out what you are doing today. Obviously, this is easier in a small organization than a large one. Just create a spreadsheet with one line for each project. Projects are not releases but discrete deliverables; it sometimes takes a while to get the correct granularity here. List how many people are on the project, how many are really needed, target release, capital and non-recurring engineering (NRE) costs, the names of people working on the project, etc. Create different types of categories so that you can analyze where you spend money. One type of category is like those listed above in the top-down budgeting discussion and another might be based on the functional areas (network protocols, virtual memory, io infrastructure, etc.) in which you are spending money.

Completing this first bottoms-up exercise gives you a good idea of where you are spending money today.

Now you have the data.

It is important that you have an agreement about the percentages to spend on the top-down budget categories from management and peers (e.g. product management, support). It is also important that you read and address the *Strategy* section of this book. The final thing you should have is a target budget from your management. You can go back and discuss those numbers with management, but you need to have all of your homework done first.

See the sample budget in the Project Example Appendix.

> 33. *Do you have a list of the projects and products your company wants you and your team to work on and a mechanism for prioritizing those products?*

Armed with the current projects, strategy, and the investment mix, engineering and product management should list all projects they want to do in the bottoms-up spreadsheet with estimates of what it is going to take to complete all of the new projects. Then product management and engineering need to develop a priority list with projects bucketed from 1 to 10 with 10 being the most important. The priorities should be based on good business practices (real value to the customer, etc.).

Prioritization can be misleading. For example, engineering may propose infrastructure projects that are critical and they mark them as a priority 10. If those projects were not on the product management list, they would be ranked below items that are moderately important to both teams. One tool you can use is to sum the squares of the priorities (so product management specific or engineering specific high priority items do not get lost).

The resulting list should be a first approximation of what projects you should do. The top down budget and the guesses should give you the opportunity to draw a line and see what can be done and what cannot. Part of the analysis should be how well the budget fits into the strategies and the top-down budget categories. If your investment profile does not match the desired investment mix, you need to either modify priorities or propose new projects that address the areas in which you want to invest. Obviously some negotiation will happen, and some projects will move above and below the line.

Some major things you should consider during this process:

- Quarterly costs. A single number for the whole year is probably not appropriate. You'll need to hit your target for each quarter.
- Hiring ramp. Assume you can hire at most one person per month per manager; hiring depends on a lot of factors. Don't budget big numbers all at once for people who are not on board already.
- Legitimize overhead costs. Things like standards committees, maintenance, compliance, etc. should all have their own rows.
- Fractions. Try to stay to at most half-person granularity. This means you have to round and adjust. Smaller than a half-person is hard to manage.
- Management. Try to bind managers into the projects. This is hard but anytime you have a row that says "management", it gets hard to fund!
- Other costs: licenses, capital equipment, consulting, etc.

Do not misconstrue a budget for a schedule commitment. Good engineering practices require some amount of design and prototyping before a schedule can be arrived at. This concept takes a lot of socialization.

> 34. Do you have a mechanism for modifying the list of projects and products your team is working on after the initial budgeting process is complete?

Try not to budget again too often. If you get more money, you should just go down the list to which you agreed. If someone wants you to do his or her project, give that person your list and ask what he or she wants to trade.

Almost everyone will object to something in the final budget. People will always want their pet project done. You have to stand firm on giving them a choice. I usually say that for the most part I am project/feature agnostic – the team agrees on the priority and executes the plan. I am also very open. I have gone through 300 line budgets with an extended group of peers. At the end they said they were depressed because they wanted more done but that we had chosen the right things within our means.

It is important that you keep track of budgets the same way you keep track of schedules. Watch and manage and adjust. It is easy to exceed your budget if you do not watch. This is as important to your company's success as other parts of your job. Take this seriously.

Hiring

> 35. Do you have a process for measuring, managing, and succeeding at hiring?

You and your team need to be successful at hiring.

Budgets should be your team's highest priority. Hiring should be your second highest priority. Without a team, you cannot accomplish your tasks.

Sometimes it is hard to make this a priority with so many tasks at hand. Unlike budgets, hiring is usually a longer and more unending process because you will have a pool to hire against and some attrition to fill. Keeping momentum and focus is more of a challenge. Do not accept excuses that people are too busy to interview or hire. Remember this is the second highest priority!

Hiring can also be hard because it is often a start-again/stop-again process. You are granted a specific headcount to hire against. You get your team going on the process. Then a freeze is called because of bad quarterly results. The company may need to restrict hiring because of fiscal constraints or to show their investors they are responding to sluggish economics and are being fiscally responsible. Either way, you have to stop hiring.

Hiring can also be hard because good people are hard to find in any economic climate. Often other companies are hiring at the same time you are hiring.

> 36. Have you taken the steps to make hiring a priority for you and your team?

All these issues make hiring frustrating and challenging. Yet it remains your second highest priority task. Take the first part of your staff meeting to review hiring status and plans. If you have an in-house recruiter, invite him or her to join your meeting for that status. Make sure that each of your direct staff members comes prepared with his or her status to that meeting. The status should include:

- How many resumes did they receive?
- How many resumes resulted in interviews?
- How many people are they forecasting to hire in the next thirty days?
- How many candidates are close to offers?
- What challenges are they seeing?

Show your team this is a priority. Treat this like a development project. Identify, assign, and follow up on action items. Attack problems and measure success.

It is important to understand hiring rates. This will help you budget, schedule projects, and adjust plans.

There are a lot of ways to find candidates. The best way is always personal referrals from existing employees. Make sure they have an incentive to refer candidates. Most companies do this with a cash bonus. Do not be stingy with the bonus as this mechanism will be more cost effective than most others, even if you are generous.

Because of the nature of hiring, use every means at your disposal to find candidates. More targeted efforts will provide more targeted results. Internet postings and job fairs do not cost a lot and they will provide a lot of resumes to sift through, but they usually provide very little return.

Skilled professional recruiters will provide much fewer resumes but the resumes may represent much better candidates. They also cost more. Here are some tips on working with recruiters:

- Find recruiters who work in your technical area.
- Take the time to explain your business and skills needs to them.
- Follow up quickly with candidates.
- Negotiate fees.
- Provide feedback so they can adjust their search.
- Do not continue a relationship if you are not getting good resumes.
- Make sure they check if the candidate really wants to leave his or her current job.

Some companies require that you use in-house recruiters in order to reduce costs. I have had good and bad experiences with both in-house and external recruiters. The important point is to find a skilled recruiter.

While finding a good resume may be the hardest part of the process, it is not the end of the process! It is easy to drop the ball at each step along the way and either make the process drag out or lose the candidate altogether.

Here are some tips for the interview and hiring process once you have a resume:

- Identify who is responsible for setting up interviews, collecting feedback, and driving the paperwork for an offer.
- Develop a time goal with your team for resume follow up: e.g. a phone screen within 48 hours.
- Develop a time goal with your team to complete interviews: e.g. interviews complete within 7 days of a successful phone screen.
- Develop a time goal for getting an offer into your candidate's hands once you decide you want to hire him or her.
- Limit the number of interviewers: e.g. to four people. It is not the number of people you pick to conduct interviews; it is the quality of the people that is important. Using too many interviewers is an inefficient use of resources and slows down the process.
- Do reference checks. There is no substitute for this. Remember that everyone has some flaws. Make sure they speak to their challenges in an interview. Even ask them what their references or people who worked with them would say.

Note that hiring a manager is different than hiring a developer. No one is anxious to hire his or her own boss. Developers may enjoy not having a manager or they might like some interim reporting situation. Developers are independent and they are discriminating. While you should not disregard their comments, do not expect overwhelming positive comments when you have developers interview their prospective managers. If you do hire over people's objections, make sure you share your rationale and set expectations around everyone making the new hire successful.

> 37. Do you and your team have processes in place to make newly hired developers successful?

Make sure that you allocate enough time and resources to making newly hired developers successful. If you do not provide these resources, you may be squandering the time and money used to hire the developer in the first place. Here are some tips:

- Provide a work environment conducive to productivity.
- Provide enough machine resources for the developer to accomplish his or her tasks.
- Identify a mentor for each new employee to answer questions and provide guidance.
- Develop and provide documentation on development conventions and products.
- Identify small tasks that the new developer can work on to learn the environment and feel accomplished quickly.

Once you have hired someone, you may find you made a mistake. Even after interviews and reference checks, you can still hire the wrong person. They might not have the skills you thought they had or they might just not fit into the organization. If the number is less than 5% then you are doing well. You may have a larger percentage when you are doing a lot of hiring. The important thing is that you recognize this and have processes to both help people succeed and, if need be, manage them out of the organization.

Layoffs

> 38. Do you have the processes and plans in place in case your company needs to layoff people in your organization?

Layoffs have become commonplace.

Layoffs are a fact of life in software organizations and just part of the tools management uses to adapt to economic changes. Therefore, we all have to understand layoffs.

Rolling layoffs are bad. Companies like Digital Equipment Corporation and Sun Microsystems, Inc. did small layoffs constantly over a number of years. This hurts morale and has people looking over their shoulders. While the intentions seem to be good (i.e. an upswing is around the corner so let's save as many of our people as we can so we will be ready), the results are usually poor.

Be aggressive with layoffs. If you have to, you can re-hire later. The mood of a group will be much better if they get to hire new folks than if they have to lay more people off later. Be careful not to binge and purge (i.e. hire a lot, layoff a lot, hire a lot, lay off a lot, etc.). Both hiring and laying people off is disruptive to an organization.

Do not spread out the pain of a layoff across an organization and expect your team to accomplish the same amount of tasks. Do not just reduce the size of each group. The first step you should do is pick projects you are not going to do and terminate those projects.

Try to retain a balanced workforce. If you only retain superstars or leaders, it may lead to more conflicts, developers boredom or reduced financial savings from the layoff.

The biggest problem that companies face is deciding what not to do. They do not want to disappoint any customer by ending the life of a product because of economic issues. Few companies realize that the choice is simple: disappoint a few customers now or disappoint them all later.

Most companies have strict processes to ensure you decide whom you lay off in a fair manner. This usually requires a business case, statistics, and an algorithm. Work with your human resources and legal departments to accomplish this fairly and legally.

Chapter 5: Schedules

A product company lives or dies by its products. If you cannot accurately predict product development schedules, you cannot go to customers and tell them about the future. That may be okay for some time if you have existing products; but if you do not have existing products or the existing products are getting antiquated, the pressure is on.

There are a lot of books that talk about project decomposition and scheduling. This chapter provides an overview of the basics you should shoot for in your organization. The section on *Form Versus Function* talks about what your tools must be capable of doing. The section on *Granularity and Milestones* talks about the content of the schedules. The chapter on *Execution* later in the book will talk more about how to manage schedules once they are in place.

Form versus Function

> 39. Do you require schedules for all of your developers?

The data is what is important.

A lot of people stand on ceremony on what tool they use for scheduling. You should be more interested in making sure there are robust schedules and reporting. While the scheduling mechanism can vary, the reporting mechanism should not.

Here are some capabilities a scheduling tool needs:

> 40. If your employees meet their schedules, can they go home at the end of the week knowing they have done a good job and completed their tasks or do they feel they need to keep working regardless?

- Per person schedules. Each person should be able to see his or her deliverables. This is how they know whether they can go home at the end of the week or should work harder. This is how they know they have accomplished something.

> 41. Have you identified all of the dependencies in your schedules (inside your group, inside your company, and outside your company)?

- Managing dependencies. Understanding interrelationships between tasks is critical and knowing the critical path is critical. This is where many projects fall short.

> **42. Do you have a mechanism for managing the schedule once it is initially complete?**

- Ongoing management. I have not found a tool that does this well. It is critical to be able to get updates from developers, apply those to the schedule and see where you are. Developers never work on one task at a time, and it is important for management and developers to get a clear picture of what is left and what changes do to the schedule.
- Tracking partially done tasks. This is tricky and you can decompose a task into design, coding, testing, review, and assign percentages; but in the end the developer must estimate how much time the remaining work will take and your tool must be able to represent these partially done tasks.
- Analysis. If you are going to reward people, hold people accountable, or work to make your organization better, it is critical to be able to analyze what happened during a project.

Reporting should be hierarchical. Each project should get information from their engineers on how they are doing against their schedules. I have tried having a "stand and deliver" meeting where engineers report in a group, but it appears to cause a lot of angst. The important thing is that the data get compiled and the schedule updated. The report should show where the project is ahead and behind.

> **43. Do you have an agreed upon tool for developing and managing schedules?**

If you have a lot of projects, it is important to have a way to report on them. Here is a standard set of items that I like to see in a report:

- Status. Is the project within its bounds (see the Strategy Chapter on boundaries)? Use red, green, yellow when red means out of bounds, green means on track, and yellow means you were not out of bounds, but there was an issue that might force it to be so.

- Accomplishments since the last report.
- Goals to be accomplished for the next report.
- Issues that would make the item yellow or red.

At Sun, my group managed over 80 projects simultaneously. We reviewed them with the management team once a month. It was not a problem-solving venue; instead it was a reporting venue. Problems were identified and taken offline to solve. We were able to do it in about two hours. The people managers were responsible for delivering these reports, and this made it clear who was responsible for the project. The meeting also served as a communication mechanism. It became clear where there were overlaps and inconsistencies.

Granularity and Milestones

> 44. Is the granularity of your schedules fine grain enough to give you early warning when your team is off-course?

You must have enough fine grain schedules to know quickly if you need to make changes.

Engineers often say software cannot be scheduled. It is not true. The first manager who taught me that software could be scheduled was Larry Weber at MIPS. He sat down with us and helped us do project decomposition. He entered the schedules and he managed them.

> 45. Have you identified the key milestones for your schedules and deliverables required to make those milestones?

There are a lot of steps to scheduling. The first is to understand milestones. There are standard sets of milestones for every project and there are unique ones for each project. Everyone has different names for different phases and milestones. Here are standard types of milestones:

- Requirements freeze. This comes from product management. They need to get to closure early in the process. Allowing this date to slip causes feature creep.
- Plan freeze. This requires a response from engineering about what they can do with resources and some negotiation back and forth with product management. You should be able to do rough estimates and draw a line (see the chapter on Budgeting).
- Design freeze. Engineering should make it clear at this point what the basic architecture is, what the user sees, and undetermined issues. Engineering should produce enough of the design specification so that product management can determine that engineering is heading in a direction that will meet requirements. There should also be enough detail at this point so that engineering leadership can determine that the project is consistent with architectural goals.
- Code freeze. This should be the end of code development. This should include unit test and code reviews.
- Alpha. Should have developed and run all tests. Enough of the functionality must work to continue integration.
- Beta. Should be FCS quality (see the section on criteria) without having had a broad field test.
- FCS. Should pass all criteria and have been through field test.

Here are some other milestones to consider:

- Screen shot freeze is when GUIs are frozen and documentation and testing can begin.
- User interface review is to review the interface of the completed end-to-end product.
- Documentation complete. This should include manuals, getting started guides, etc.

- Schedule checkpoint is when you will know more about the development process to reassess where you are.
- Feature checkpoint. Sometimes the market changes as you are developing and you need to adjust.
- Late feature binding. Sometimes you can test most of a product and add a cordoned off piece after Alpha or Beta. This should not be done for fundamental pieces of the product.

Once you have your list of milestones, you can start scheduling the initial pieces through the design freeze. Many times you can adjust to surprises in the requirements, but there are times you need to reschedule. Early phases are usually done by senior developers. It is hard to schedule the whole project before you get through that phase. It is also hard to get out of design and planning phases, so manage it closely.

Once you know what you are building, then you can schedule. The following are some guidelines for scheduling:

> *46. Does your schedule have discreet deliverables that enable you to determine that a task in a schedule is both complete and correct?*

- Tasks in a schedule must have real measurable working deliverables. Sometimes this means creating scaffolding to see if the code works. Sometimes it means re-ordering tasks so they can be measured. If you do not do this, the job will be larger when you integrate. It delays your ability to really know where you are in a project and often leads to schedule pressure which often leads to cutting corners. For example never have a task that says "Coded reconnect feature". Instead have "Coded and tested and checked-in reconnect feature".
- Individual tasks should be no larger than two weeks in duration. Try to keep them to one week.

- Only schedule 4 days a week. This leaves time for meetings, budget fixing, etc. It is hard not to play games and take a week task down to four days. If a task is a five-day task, make sure you allocate five days.
- Take vacations and holidays into account.
- Help the team with decomposition. Use standard techniques like the number of lines, interfaces, comparing to previously completed tasks, etc.
- Limit the number of partially completed tasks you allow a developer to be working on simultaneously. The more partially completed tasks, the harder it is to predict the completion of any of them; and therefore it is hard to predict the completion of your project. If one of those partially completed tasks does run into trouble, you won't know until it is late in the project. If developers do complete tasks more or less in order, you know those pieces are done and it does not add risk into the later part of the schedule. Ignore complaints about inefficiencies; predictability will more than compensate for inefficiencies.
- Require automated unit testing by development engineers (see the section on *Quality Assurance*). They cannot say their testing is done with hand testing.

See the sample schedule in the Project Example Appendix.

47. Do you have buy-in from your developers for their schedules?

Make sure you have buy-in from your engineers. If you do not have buy-in, you will not succeed. Make sure they allocate enough time for design and integration. Make sure you believe the schedule. Make sure everyone understands that success or failure of your group and potentially the company rides on their doing their part. Make sure you define adjustment points where you re-calibrate with engineering and your management.

48. Have you communicated the schedule throughout the company?

Once you have a schedule, you need to identify the stakeholders and communicate the schedule to them. Be completely open and honest about assumptions and risks.

Communicate how you are going to manage the schedule, report status, and deal with change.

Chapter 6: Execution

As noted in the chapter on *Schedules*, companies live or die on the availability of their products. That chapter was about setting up the schedules. If you take the product definition and the schedules and the status you can get a picture of where you are with product development, but now what do you do?

This chapter talks about what you do as things change in the section on *Auditing Progress*. It then goes on to discuss what you have to do as an organization to get better at what you do over time in the section on *Continuous Improvement*. Finally we discuss a little about what to do with the information about progress in *Marketing Yourself and Your Group*.

Auditing progress

> 49. Do you have a process to manage when a project or product goes off course?

It is critical to keep track and adjust resources, schedules, features, etc. all the time.

One of the longest termed chairmen of the United States Federal Reserve, Alan Greenspan, continuously fussed with interest rates, adjusting based on changing events. You must do the same with projects. You will learn new things everyday:

- The designs were not accurate.
- The specifications were not accurate.
- The market changes requiring a new feature.
- Your schedule did not provide enough time for integration.
- A third party is not delivering their parts on time or with quality.
- Your key engineer gets sick and is out for two critical weeks.
- An engineer on whom you depend for a piece of code is not capable of doing the work.
- An engineer leaves the company.

Lots of things happen to make a project go out of bounds. The boundaries that you can adjust are well known:

- Features
- Quality
- Resources
- Schedule

You cannot go back to the well and adjust the same boundary all the time without causing grave consequences to your company:

- If you remove too many features, you will not have a competitive product.
- If you add too many features, you will not make your dates.
- If you scrimp on quality, you will get a bad reputation.
- If you wait until the product is perfect, you will miss the market window.
- If you make your engineers work extra hours all the time, they will burn out.
- If you add too many resources, you can run out of money.
- If you slip the schedule, you will make it hard for your sales folks to sell and you might miss a market window.

The Greeks said, "Everything in moderation." This is a good place to remind you of my words in the introduction: apply moderation and judgment here.

> 50. Do you have a mechanism to track why your projects and products go off course?

First, you must pay attention and get the facts. Someone should be collecting schedule data each and every week. It doesn't matter who does this as long as you can roll robust data up and expose problem areas. You must drive an action plan on each of the problem areas. Your tools are listed above. Constant attention is the way to manage it.

Rarely can you change one thing without another. In one company I made an awful mistake with one of my team's projects. We had learned that our design was inadequate for specific situations, and we had to architect and engineer a fundamental underlying piece of the product for a second time late in the project. The CTO was driving it and we agreed not to change our dates and see what happens. I knew better. Sure enough we had a two-month slip at the end because critical resources were busy working on that instead of fixing bugs.

To makes things worse, I allowed that project to have almost no integration time in order to make some goal dates. This, too, was a mistake. You can cut corners in planning, but it will catch up to you in the end. Do the right thing up front.

It is important that you keep your eye on the ball. The frequency with which you examine status depends on the size of the organization, the quality of your staff, and where you are in a release cycle. Finishing a project usually requires daily meetings as you approach code complete and those meetings might continue on and off through FCS.

> 51. Have you identified who is responsible for tracking status of products and projects?

As always, it is important that you identify who will track status. Depending on how your company and your organization work, this may be a manager or program manager with direct or indirect management responsibilities for the developers on the project. Make sure it is clear who collects the data, how it is rolled up, and who is responsible for identifying and implementing changes.

Continuous Improvement

> 52. Do you have a process for improving your organization based on ongoing experience?

If you cannot effect change and learn how to be better, your organization will not be taking advantage of its full potential.

There are a lot of well-defined programs you can adopt to help improve your organization. Most involve three main components:

- Measuring and analyzing a company's processes.
- Determining how those processes impact customers and hence revenue.

- Implementing change to address any issues found.

While established programs to help institute change are not a substitute for leadership, they can help both jumpstart an improvement initiative and provide a proven framework. If you do adopt an existing program, make sure to customize it for your organization. Some people who get involved tend to become zealots, and it is best to remember that these tools are meant to serve your organization and not the other way around.

Here are some of the well-known programs, and you can search any online bookstore for books to help you with these programs:

- Six Sigma
- Balanced Scorecard
- Customer Driven Organizations

I will attempt to identify the key things I think are important to help you make your organization better. The important thing is that you put some program in place to do so. It matters less which one, if any, you choose.

Here is my basic list:

- Define what is important to you. You cannot solve all problems at once. Pick your battles. Start with three items. This also requires you have a strategy for the company (see the chapter on *Strategy*) so that your improvement efforts align with the strategy.
- Figure out how to measure results. One of the cool things about Six Sigma is that it gives you tools to measure things that you might think are very subjective. Many times items you need to measure are obvious (making schedules on time, reducing time to delivering bug fixes, reducing rework, etc.) but some are not (effectiveness of marketing programs, effectiveness of bundled products, etc.).

- Put someone in charge. See the chapter on *Roles and Responsibilities*. It is very important that one person is on the hook for driving improvement and has the authority to drive it.
- Make sure everyone knows that improving the company is a priority. If you do not legitimize time to do this work, it won't get done. People who are in the firing line for putting out products will always defer other work. This has to be measured and rewarded in the review and compensation programs.
- Follow up. It is important to keep track of an improvement effort and to support changes in the organization to make improvements and to measure again!

A simple example of this was an effort to determine which bugs end up in escalations at Sun. Part of this effort was to determine what bugs got fixed in releases and what bugs were carried over and whether any of the bugs that got carried over ended up as customer escalations. We found out that people were fixing some of the lower priority bugs and leaving some of the higher priority bugs. It was clear that we needed to plan and prioritize people's work to deal with higher priority bugs.

Another example of working to make our team better at Sun was education for incoming employees. During the tech boom we had at times hired 25 people in one group from a company that was laying off people. I assigned a program manager to manage this effort. We ended up with both live and taped classes, mentor programs, and people coming up to speed much quicker and accreting value for the company.

Marketing Yourself and Your Group

> 53. Do you communicate both success and failures to your key stakeholders on a regular basis?

You have to let people know what you are doing.

This goes back to when you were taught to do your own work in school. This goes back to being taught not to brag. Some people have real resistance to telling other folks what is going on – good news, bad news, and just plain news.

The best way to get better rewards for your group is to tell people outside your organization what good things they are doing. This may be a simple email or it may entail sitting down with someone else in the company and sharing some incident -- the more often the better.

I have had many managers working for me that needed to improve in this area. I would go by their office and demand they send mail before the end of the day regarding some subject. At times, people thought those managers were not performing well and in reality no one knew what they were doing because they were not communicating. The impression of people who are reluctant to communicate can improve rapidly with a little communication.

The biggest lament I would get is that it seems like bragging. I tell them to look at it as communication. It cannot hurt.

The same thing is true for things that go wrong. The best way to mitigate the effect of bad news is to deliver the bad news yourself. Own up to the bad news. Take responsibility for something that went wrong. State how you are going to handle it. If someone else delivers the bad news, the impact will be worse for you and your team.

54. Have you identified the key stakeholders for your product or project?

Part of the process of communicating news requires identifying who are the stakeholders for your product or project. Who really cares and who is affected? If you don't involve people who really care, there is a great chance for them to second-guess your plans. If you don't include groups who are affected, they will be surprised and may not be prepared to do their part.

Sometimes groups who are affected by a product or project may not care about the project because they might be busy doing something else, but you must persevere. One mechanism you can use for project information is to create a sign-off sheet for each phase of your project. Although the sign-off sheet is not a replacement for the social aspect of this process, it can heighten a group's interest in doing their part; and it accomplishes the task of communication.

Chapter 7: Development Processes

It is clear that one of the key factors in the success of a group is setting up appropriate processes that help your team define, develop, release, and support a product. The first section in this chapter discusses the process of developing *Processes*. This is important.

Once I have that groundwork, I discuss product *Criteria* which helps define when a product is done. I then go on to tactical items including *Source Code Control, Release Models* and *Managing Bugs*. This should give some of the basics on the infrastructure you need in place to develop a successful team and produce quality products.

Processes

> 55. Do you have a well-defined set of processes for development so new developers can succeed quickly?

Implement processes cautiously.

From the moment there is even one person in an organization, processes are required: coding conventions, testing conventions, etc.

As organizations grow, more processes will be required: project proposals, interface taxonomies, internationalization, etc.

Processes, however, are not free. They require thought, agreement, documentation, implementation, and auditing. They are also the cause for people to feel that organizations are too bureaucratic and make them feel less effective. Processes are ways for organizations to be more effective, but they do not necessarily make individuals more effective.

The following are some good things to think about processes:

> 56. Do your development processes account for exceptional situations?

- Make sure processes account for exceptions. Make sure exceptions happen rarely.
- If exceptions happen too frequently, either the organization needs to change its behavior so it submits fewer exceptions, or the process needs to change because it does not adequately account for the behavior represented by the exception (which is supposed to occur rarely).

- Make sure to develop processes that require work appropriate to the situation. Implement a fast track version of each process (e.g. email approval of small projects instead of a full blown steering committee review).

Look at the sections on *Messages and Rules* and on *Rationale*. Processes are rules. Make sure that you explain why you are implementing a process and communicate it to the troops. Ask their input on what they might suggest instead. Stick to requirements: e.g. "The company needs TCP/IP Version 6 to be a success and we need a way to ensure all products can handle TCP/IP Version 6; so we are instituting a process to ensure that happens."

Criteria

> 57. Do you have well defined criteria for accepting a product at each stage of development?

If you cannot measure something, you cannot make it better.

A criteria document is one of your greatest tools. This is a single spreadsheet with all of the criteria required to accept a product. Avoid having the criteria only consist of having no showstopper bugs. A bug list can represent other issues like test failures, etc., but it is not a concise description of what the product has to do to be released.

The spreadsheet should include rows for each criteria item including:

- Item Description
- Unit
    - What the goal is measured in (e.g. pass/fail, percent complete, queries per second, etc.)
- Goal

100 Questions to Ask Your Software Organization 77

- o A goal for that item (say queries per second and the goal being 1000). You may want an actual and a minimum where you can live with the minimum but you need eventually to get to the actual.
- Baseline
  - o Value of the first ever run
- Last Run
- Current Run
- Notes
  - o This might have scenarios or premises for testing criteria.

The following is an outline for the sections of the spreadsheet:

- Features
  - o List major features with percent completion.
- Testing
  - o This should include the number of tests expected to be written/running for an area.
  - o Tests should include things like cockpit tests, functional tests, interface tests, performance tests, stress tests, interoperability tests, configuration tests, wall-clock tests, etc.
  - o Each test or group of tests should have a result. The granularity will depend on your situation.
- Licensing
  - o This includes handling copyrights, export-licenses, royalties, notices, etc.
- Certification
  - o UL, FCC, Dolby, etc.

This should help drive schedules, test development, and resource allocation. It also will help in marketing the product, as it will provide input to collateral documentation.

In the early days of a release, you may have to have dates when a criteria item will be delivered. You may not require all items by Alpha or Beta.

The agreement around the content should be coordinated with product management. Product management should infuse input from the field, support, and the competition.

Having this process and this data helps sell to customers. They like to know you are measuring things. This would be key input for an ISO® 9000 or CMM® effort.

See the sample criteria in the Project Example Appendix.

Source code control

> 58. Do you have a single source code control tool?

Do not underestimate the importance of source code control!

Source code control is the set of processes and tools you and your team use to archive and retrieve source code for your product.

Prioritize function over form. People can find it easier to use one tool or another. One tool may have features that suit a particular situation. If you stand on ceremony about which tool to use, you may miss out on productivity gains or developer satisfaction. Pick whatever tool suits your environment, but pick one tool.

Here are the top things you need to do with source code control:

- Make it easy to use. If you make it hard to use, people will avoid it and work around it.
- Think about remote access. If you have folks overseas or in remote sites, make sure you think about how this will work. If you have partners that need access, think about that.

- Branching and merging. There should be reasonable tools to do this. There will be times you need to do three-way merges and reasonable tools are available to help you.
- Atomic check-ins. It is important to be able to check in files that are dependent on each other and be able to identify them. You may have to remove them and having this grouping ability is important.

> **59. Do you have processes and tools that help you manage multiple simultaneous releases?**

- Multiple releases. You will have to support multiple releases. Make sure you are set up to do this. Your tools should support being able to recreate the sources and tools used to build a release in the field. They should also support making changes to the sources and then applying them to other releases.

> **60. Do you have processes that minimize regressions from release to release?**

- If you want to avoid regressions, institute a policy that requires you to save the changes in the latest release first and then backport and save those changes to older versions as required. By always making sure the newer versions of software have all the changes your organization makes, you insure that no customer will get a change in an older version of software and then lose it when they upgrade to a newer version. This is not free but well worth it.

> **61. Do you have processes and tools that can limit changes to a product as you get close to release?**

- Check-in restrictions. As you get closer to a release, fewer people and fewer source code check-ins should occur. Things like multiple code reviews or manager approval are items that help do this, and some tools provide this support.

Release Models

> 62. Do you have a train based release model?

Trains are the only way to go!

The two basic models of doing releases are the big release model and the train model. The big release model has a large release (usually planned once every 6+ months) with a lot of features. The train model has a periodic release (every 4 or fewer months) with fewer features. The train model treats releases as managed processes, rather than one-time events.

The advantages of the train model are numerous:

- If one feature in a train release is delayed, the reminder of the features can be released and the tardy feature can be added in the next (coming-soon) release.
- Fewer changes are easier to manage.
- Customers can depend on when a release gets out.
- It is easier to adapt to customer requirements, as the next release is not far away.
- It is easier to match revenue periods.
- It pulls a lot of pressure off releases to shove in one more feature or bug fix.
- Developers are motivated to get on a train, and they do not have to wait a long time to release their product if they have to miss one.

I have used the train model in every product since 1996. We produced a release every 90 days with features in Solaris without a single meltdown. While it may take some adjustment as you start this process, each release gets more efficient and smoother if you adhere to the train model.

At Sun, the decision on how Solaris releases would work was my first decision in steering Solaris. The team was only going to allow features in every other quarterly release; but it became very clear that if the Software group didn't allow features every 90 days, the hardware groups would produce their feature releases on their own (which is what they were doing). Having one release train also helped the support organization because there were never special releases to handle special situations since the product was released frequently enough to alleviate those issues.

When I first rolled this train model out at Sun, we had layered products that went on top of Solaris and were built, sold, and released separately (e.g. a web package). The thought at the time was that the layered packages could move quicker and release more often. We had a big discussion because some core feature that belonged in Solaris was being shoehorned into one of the layered packs because Solaris was too slow with releases. After a year it became clear that the Solaris team could deliver faster and more reliably than any other vehicle in Sun. In fact Solaris became the delivery vehicle or limo ride for Java™, IPlanet™, Oracle's database and other software needed by Solaris customers. It eventually begot Sun's big Java Enterprise System project that put all of their products on the train model.

Making a release train work and employing the discipline to keep it on time takes leadership. It requires good processes like a well-defined cycle and mechanisms for determining what could leave on what train (quality and priority), etc.

Managing Bugs

> **63. Do you have a bug management tool in your company?**

Managing bugs may be the most single critical thing that will decide your group's success.

You must determine where bugs come from. If you do not do this, you are doomed to repeat mistakes. Rework is expensive no matter where it is caught. The later it is caught, the more expensive it is. It might involve a customer and require your sales force or support organizations to get involved; you may lose the customer, other software components may become dependent on that behavior, and any change might cause a ripple effect, etc.

> 64. Does your bug tracking system allow you to express the severity of the bug, when it needs to be fixed, and what the customer thinks is the importance of the bug?

Here are some basic blocking and tackling things:

- Make sure a test is created for each bug you fix where possible. There is nothing worse than a regression. The cost of finding a bug twice (customer impact, support, diagnosis, etc.) far outweighs the cost of developing a regression test.
- Mark the reason that the bug occurred when it is closed (specification issues, design issue, coding issue, etc.).
- Prioritize bugs by when they need to be fixed. You can use release and priority. Priority 1 has to be fixed, priority 2 can be fixed, and priority 3 is an enhancement.
- Provide a way to describe objectively what the customer experience is. This is usually done with a severity number. Severity 1 is a machine crash, feature failure, data corruption, or security problem; severity 2 is a partial feature failure; severity 3 is an annoyance; severity 4 is an enhancement.
- Provide a way to describe how important the customer feels it is. This is often overlooked as data but is critical and removes overloading the priority field above. This can be customer C1 meaning the customers feels it is critical and needs a patch; C2 should be fixed in the next release, etc.

It is common to try to address customer desires or what is good for the product and not both simultaneously. In most companies there is huge competition for engineering resources and discussions need to occur that trade off new projects and fixing bugs. Only by collecting the above data can a team make any tradeoff. It usually takes product management, customer support, and engineering to make those decisions.

The bug list is also how you manage the end game of big projects. From the minute you hit code freeze, the rest is managed by the bug list. You need to use the same discipline as you would for a released product. If a bug would cause a patch, it should be fixed. Otherwise, you have to look at each fix for a bug being as likely to cause new bugs as to just fixing the original.

> **65. Do you have tools and processes in place that help you manage bug trends and rates?**

In the phases after code freeze, it is critical to track the bug trend. If the incoming rate for critical bugs does not trend towards zero and if the fix rate is much slower than the incoming rate, your product is not ready. The exact numbers will depend on the size and complexity of the product.

It is also critical to have milestones in your schedule where you treat bugs differently. At a certain point, you need to say that any new bugs that wouldn't stop shipment of a product will just go into the first patch. If you do not do this, you may iterate forever and never release a product.

Clearly you must meet your criteria (see the section on Criteria), and too many bugs will reduce the effectiveness of any product. All software products go out with bugs. Your team needs to decide what is acceptable for your customer base. If you are selling a product that is expected to run 7x24 and is a critical service for the customer, the requirements will be different than a non-critical browser based application that can be easily restarted.

As always you must identify owners for different parts of the bug process including:

- Who tracks the bugs?
- Who makes priority decisions?
- Who fixes a bug?
- Who approves a fix?
- Who verifies a fix?

Chapter 8: Remote Management

Remote Management has become a big challenge over the last two decades. If you have not yet done so, you probably will experience remote management in the future.

This chapter goes through some of the basics in the section entitled *Why Do It?* in which I talk about motivations and some high level guidance on remote sites. I then move on to a section called *Center of Gravity* that talks about main site versus non-main site interactions, politics and strategies. I spend some time in the *Care and Feeding* section talking about what will help make those remote sites be happy and successful. Finally I detail some of the basics of what you need to do to run a remote site in the *How To Do It* section.

Why Do It?

> 66. Have you identified why are you doing remote management?

It is always more efficient to have all developers in one site.

It is important to take some time to understand why you have remote organizations, as it will help you plan and be more successful with them.

There are a lot of reasons that organizations have remote sites: cost savings, acquisitions, talent pools, cost of living, and evolution.

During expansion times, it is not easy to find talent, and it is important not to lose opportunities because you cannot find engineers. A lot of remote sites open during boom times only to close or consolidate when things get tough. This is a normal part of a business cycle and it is not necessarily a bad thing for the company. It is useful to acknowledge it.

You have to come to a decision as to whether you want remote sites or not. Once you do, there are some basic blocking and tackling things you can do to help make the remote team successful:

> 67. Do you have a communication plan in place for remote sites?

- Develop a communication plan. How will managers, project managers, and engineers interact and communicate with the remote team (one-on-ones, team meetings, visits, etc.)? Put a plan together and track it. See the section on *Venues* in the chapter on *Communication* for more ideas on how to proceed.
- Identify who owns making the remote site successful. Empower them and hold them accountable for that success. This can be someone at that site or someone at your main site. You will need leadership in both places.

- Create joint projects for people working in remote sites and the main site. First impulse is to do the opposite and cordon off responsibilities. Do not isolate remote sites or you will get huge anti-bodies and resistance to anything the remote site develops. It has to be one team.

> **68. Do you support extensive travel between sites?**

- If you can't afford the travel, do not do remote development. There is no substitute for face time. I have seen reports that claim that body language constitutes between 55% and 90% of communication. You cannot see body language remotely.
- Understand and acknowledge the differences. Cultures, work habits, languages, time zones, compensation may all be different. If you ignore it or keep it quiet, resentments can build.

Center of Gravity

> **69. Have you created teams that integrate developers from your remote site and your main corporate site?**

It is important to know where the center of gravity is for your team.

The fact that decisions are made and hallway conversations take place at the main site affects the remote site's ability to succeed. Acknowledge it. Do not try to be egalitarian because it does not reflect reality. Instead you should try to compensate for it. Make sure your management understands this. I was in one situation where upper management was not located at the developer center of gravity, and it caused significant problems resulting in eventually changing the center of gravity by laying off most of the developers in the remote site and expanding the team where upper management resided.

A good example of combining teams was at Sun where the company had made an acquisition of a team in Los Angeles that became part of the Solaris team. The developers at headquarters always looked at that team with disdain. Whatever source code they tried to check in got extra scrutiny and frequently got rejected. There was an "us vs. them" attitude. I got lucky because by chance one of the projects required a joint team. It was a successful project for Solaris and promoted more understanding between the groups. There were more visits and phone calls between developers at each of the sites. The best part was that in the end, the teams thought better of each other enabling them to collaborate on other projects.

After this, I required that all remote teams have some aspects of joint development with developers at our main offices. If there were battles or tough discussions to be had, they could be done between developers at the main offices where some subset of them represented remote team members. Hence, it became a proxy mechanism for hallway conversations. It brought new people up to speed more quickly and reduced the barriers for acceptance of product developed (now partially) by remote teams.

Care and Feeding

> 70. Does your remote team feel like they are a valued part of the company?

Remote sites will always have a tendency to feel like they are second-class citizens.

You will have to go out of your way to make them feel heard and feel that the company wants them. You should care that the remote site feels good about the work they are doing.

Take the time to over-communicate with remote sites. When you visit a remote site, make sure you and/or your managers take remote teams out to lunch or dinner. Take turns between taking out individuals and groups (teams, junior engineers, senior engineers, etc.). Give them an extra chance to feel comfortable with telling you about problems.

In your main office, you get a chance to see people on a regular basis. You can ask how it is going at the coffee station or the lunchroom. You can't do that with remote employees.

> **71. Is there a manager at your remote sites that can help local developers even if the developers do not report to them?**

Make sure there is a local technical manager on whom your developers can rely at the remote site. Even if your developers do not report to that local manager, it is helpful when they don't have access to their own manager who may be remote. This helps bridge the gap between visits, and helps address issues that may arise in a more timely fashion.

Many times remote sites are the first to be let go when there are financial problems. This is the way it is. I always told developers at remote sites that their contributions would help determine whether they survive in tough times. The best thing that they could do was to deliver.

How to Do It

> **72. Do you have technical and managerial leadership at the remote site?**

The first critical piece to make a remote site successful is to have an anchorperson. You need someone who will be the soul of the site and ensure its success. This is not always the site manager – you may have someone who manages logistics or even human resources. This is not always a manager; sometimes it is a senior developer or program manager. This is someone who encourages people at that site. This is the person that evangelizes that site. This is the person who makes the site a success.

> **73. Do you have plans to provide challenging work for your remote team?**

Another big issue is making sure the developers at a remote site have challenging work to do. It might be attractive for developers at the corporate site to think they can hand the less interesting work to folks at a remote site, but it becomes hard to retain good developers in that kind of scheme. This also implies that you need to bring in developers who are qualified to do more challenging work. Having challenging work to do will make the remote site more productive and provide tangible growth goals for more junior members of a remote team.

You also need the following things:

> **74. Is your company committed to having remote sites?**

- Buy in from corporate. Without this you will hit roadblocks at each turn.
- Develop a talent pool. If you can't grow the team or replace members who leave, the site will die. It is good to make friends with the local university and even start an intern program.
- Understand the logistics: acquiring/managing a site, its infrastructure, hiring people, local laws, etc.

> **75. Do you have effective tools for communications and development at remote sites?**

- Provide tools including high quality phones and phone lines, local servers, enough Internet bandwidth to communicate with corporate effectively, etc.
- Prepare a game plan on how to hire and train your remote employees. Find a way for them to accomplish tasks for the company quickly.
- Travel in both directions. I know I said this earlier but it is worth repeating.

> **76. Do you measure the effectiveness and track issues with remote sites?**

- Treat remote development sites like another development project: set goals, track issues, identify owners, etc.

> **77. Have you allocated enough time and resources to train your team?**

- Develop a great training plan so that remote engineers can both feel part of the team and become productive quickly.
- Develop well-defined development processes.

You can kickstart remote sites by hiring whole teams. Sometimes another company may layoff or disenfranchise a team, opening an opportunity for you to employ a team that is competent and knows how to work together. It is important to have someone from corporate on the ground in the remote site from the time you embark on an endeavor like hiring a whole team until the time they start coding. It is easy to lose momentum.

When doing this overseas, you can also jump start this process by contracting or partnering with local corporations. India even has a three-letter acronym for this: BTO – buy, transfer, own.

> **78. Who is the executive sponsor for your remote site?**

It is important to identify someone on your company's executive team who will be a sponsor for a site. This is a similar concept to having joint teams discussed above – if you do not have someone from the executive team who is the champion for the site, it will be harder for the site to succeed. You need someone at budget and planning and status meetings to support and laud the remote site.

Chapter 9: Offshoring

This chapter is really a special case of Remote Management. Many of us have experience managing offshore. It is a fact of life in the software industry. I take some time in this chapter to discuss *Why Do It* but the bulk of the information on how to do it is in the previous chapter.

Why Do It?

> **79. Have you identified why you are doing development offshore?**

The cost of offshoring is much more than the salaries of your employees or contractors there. It includes equipment, travel, efficiency, etc.

The first thing I ask people who want to do offshoring is why they want to do it. Most will say cost savings and some will say they were told to do so. Offshoring is not easy.

The challenges include:

- Time zone differences
- Language differences
- Skill sets mismatches
- Finding the right talent
- Retaining the right talent
- Management
- Culture mismatches

Your mileage may vary but you should expect at least 6 months ramp time for application development and 12 months for systems development before you accrete real value from these investments.

> **80. If you have not started offshore development, have you done a cost/benefit analysis and looked at alternatives?**

You cannot expect a huge multiple initially in payback because it may take two or three offshore developers to do the work of one local developer until they really come up to speed. Even then, their lack of locality can cause inefficiencies.

Make sure you look at the requirements of any remote management situation from the chapter on *Remote Management*.

Take a look at the costs and alternatives. If you are just trying to reduce costs, you can look at other means to do so. Here are some examples:

- Outsourcing
- Hire less experienced people (interns, new graduates, etc.)
- Near shoring (other locations in your own or nearby countries)
- Improved efficiency

Sometimes there is cachet in having an off-shoring operation. You cannot fight this kind of belief because it is a religious battle.

I have had great success in starting and running offshore sites. I know there are both successful and failed offshore efforts in the industry. If you set your expectations and your management's expectations appropriately you will increase your chances for success.

> 81. Have you identified who at your corporate site will be responsible for that team's success?

You need to pick someone at your corporate site that is responsible for your offshore team's success even if they do not manage the site from day to day.

From here it is just a harder version of *Remote Management*.

Chapter 10: Humanity

It is easy to forget that you and the people to whom you report and the people who report to you and your peers are human beings. It is easy to get caught in the throes of business and forget there is more.

This chapter tries to remind you of some of the basics. *Make Them Feel Heard* talks about listening. *Accomplishment* talks about motivation. The *Reviews* section presents information about the feedback process. *Success* talks about winning. *Do the Right Thing* speaks for itself. *Compensation* discusses how important rewards are to employees, and *Empathy* speaks to how we relate to each other.

Make Them Feel Heard

> **82. Do your employees feel that you listen to them?**

I once heard it said that the difference between listening to someone versus hearing someone is whether you make him or her feel heard. Although this is not the definition of listening, the concept is worthy.

I must admit this is one of my biggest personal challenges. I move very quickly and this process takes time.

When I was managing the Solaris team, I did about one re-organization per year. It usually occurred after the budget was approved. We made adjustments to new goals and headcount targets. My staff and I would sit down and decide what was important to our team and then put proposals together. I always had some goals that were fixed like maximum headcount per manager and some that were unique each year: e.g. organizing around new initiatives. Usually everyone had to compromise on something to get to resolution. We had gone through the whole process and one person who worked for me was extremely unhappy and felt I was not listening to him. I called in a professional coach to help. The coach asked some questions and then asked that person and me to state the other's position. I did so easily. My employee was shocked. He had felt I had not a clue. I just never made him feel heard. Afterwards, he was still not happy, but he accepted the plan.

> **83. Do you employ techniques to ensure that employees know you understand their points of view?**

You have to take the time to allow for discussion. At times you have to go around the room and ask people individually what they have to say. You have to have one-on-ones. You have to practice active listening. You have to repeatedly acknowledge people. It is time consuming. It is the only way to get buy-in and engender loyalty.

I heard a therapist once define it this way: some people look at the end result or tactical resolution of an issue as success, and other people look at the process of getting to that result as the measure of success. The truth is you need both. It is easy for scientists who think in black and white to forget the latter.

Accomplishment

> **84. Do your employees feel accomplished?**

The only thing that drives employees is accomplishment.

Things like compensation and good commutes and stock options are interesting things, but they are byproducts. The thing that satisfies employees is accomplishment. All good things emanate from it. The company can be successful. The employees can feel they are done and did a good job. The employees can get a good review and a raise. The company can do well by selling the product and the stock can be worth something.

If the company does well or employees get a raise when they are not accomplishing, their position is precarious. They will not be motivated or loyal or both, and they may begin to look at rewards as entitlements regardless of their performance or the company's performance.

I always tell managers who have new employees to give them small tasks when they start working no matter how junior or senior they are. If they go off and do not accomplish something quickly, it is easy for them to have buyer's remorse or set a bad pattern of not accomplishing tasks for the company.

> **85. Do you acknowledge your employees on a regular basis both in private and in public?**

Take the time to acknowledge people. Find something good about someone in your organization each day. Tell them about it. Take the time at group meetings to acknowledge good work of people in your team. Do not worry about how big the item is; small good things deserve recognition too. Try to distribute acknowledgements where appropriate.

The act of acknowledgement has more power than you might realize. Many people grow up in environments where they did not get acknowledgement. It makes it hard for them to receive or deliver acknowledgements. You must show by example and build a culture where this is expected and is part of the norm.

Reviews

> **86. Do you and your organization do reviews on time?**

Try to remember how you felt when you were an engineer getting a review.

Reviews are important to both management and to developers. Finishing reviews late or not doing them is an insult to your developers and a risk to your company. Require that managers complete their reviews before their own ratings are determined. If the managers do not complete their employee's reviews on time, it should affect those manager's own review ratings.

General guidance on reviews follows:

> **87. Do your reviews contain concrete examples?**

- Do not provide generalities. If you cannot provide specific examples, do not bring up an issue.

- Do not surprise your employees. If you haven't talked with them throughout the year about an issue, do not bring it up for the first time at review time.
- Tell your employees how your company's grading systems work, where they are with respect to being proficient at their current grade, and what it takes to get to the next one.

88. Do you get peer feedback for your employee's reviews?

- Get input from co-workers.
- Get input from your employee and point out any discrepancies between their own self-evaluation and your evaluation of them. If they learn more of what and how you think, they are more likely to self-improve over time.

I like short reviews. Long tomes are hard to produce and hard to read. I like the following sections:

- Ratings on things that are important
- Accomplishments and strengths
- Things to improve on
- Overall rating

I like the ratings section to be graded from -5 to 5. If the employees are doing what they are supposed to do, it is a par or 0. If they are making a negative impact, it is a negative number. If they perform perfectly in that area, they get a 5. I rate hard. I like the ratings to indicate that human interaction is the most important thing to consider. I usually pick the following as things I rate:

- Technical prowess
- Execution
- Interaction
- Communication
- Leadership

> 89. Do your reviews stress interaction skills enough (versus technical skills)?

Three and a half items in the above list have to do with how you interact with people.

You have to do reviews regardless of whether there is a compensation review or not.

> 90. Do you follow through on tough messages in reviews when necessary?

One thing that is very hard is when you provide feedback, it usually takes more detail to explain areas to be improved than it does for accomplishments. It is easy for employees to take this personally. At the very least, you need to acknowledge this.

It is very hard for some managers to confront employees who are not performing as well as they should be performing. You need to encourage, train, and support your managers in this process.

Encourage your employees to respond in writing to reviews. It should not be an affront to you.

Make sure you follow up with a development plan. At Sun in the Solaris group, we required that all developers who were almost ready for a promotion have a written development plan after their last review but before the promotion. At the next review cycle we would check on the results of that plan before the actual promotion.

Success

> 91. Does your company feel like your employees are successful, and do you and your company make your employees feel successful?

Look at sports as a model for success.

This section is really more about failure than success. Baseball players are gods if they have a better than 30% rate for hits. We are taught from first grade to get 100% on our tests. We become engineers and our code either works or doesn't, and often there is not a lot of gray. Then we become managers and cannot be graded in the same way.

If every time someone left an organization to take another job a manager felt abject failure, nothing would get done! If you hit 75% success rate as a manager with all the things you have to deal with including personnel, releases, design, processes, etc., you are doing an amazing job.

As I said in the introduction, I have made plenty of mistakes. The issue is how you respond. If you look at problems as just things to be solved, you will be more successful.

Do the Right Thing

> 92. Do you accommodate special situations for good employees?

You need to feel that you are doing the right thing as a human being.

I would rather be unemployed than to do the wrong thing as a human being. This is not to say that I do not have my foibles and this is not to say that I do not make mistakes, but I try to think about how I would want to be treated when I deal with others. The biblical "Do unto others ..." applies double for managers.

Managers are asked every day to make business decisions. Some are very hard like managing people out of jobs they are not qualified to do or laying people off when tough economic times hit a company, etc. We have a choice on how we approach the issues above as well as other day-to-day issues with employees such as hardships in their families like illness or death.

> **93. Do you behave compassionately?**

Here are some basics:

- Tell the truth. Clearly there are times when there is company-restricted or personal information, but you should be as complete in your communication as you can be.
- Retain employees. It is hard and costly to get new employees.
- Communicate clearly. Take the time to figure out how to roll out information.

Bend over backwards to help well-performing employees take time off or work remotely to accommodate hardships or needs. These employees, in turn, become more loyal and are more likely to go above and beyond for you. Other employees will see this as an indication of what the company might do for them, and this may, in turn, increase their loyalty as well.

Compensation

> **94. Do you have a well-defined compensation plan?**

Never treat your employees' compensation casually.

They do not treat their compensation casually. You should not either. It may have been a while since you were living hand to mouth or restricted such that you couldn't buy the car you want or take the vacation you want or go out to lunch when you want. Your employees are probably not in the same compensation position as you are. When thinking about reducing salaries or not paying someone's bonus, think about it twice. You send a real message when you reduce or delay compensation; it may not be the message you intend. Be very careful on this subject.

> **95. Do you differentiate between compensation that is meant as a reward for the past, ongoing remuneration for the present, and incentives for the future?**

I believe there are three kinds of compensation:

- Day-to-Day. This includes salary and benefits.
- Retrospective rewards. This includes bonuses and profit sharing.
- Forward-Looking rewards. This includes stock options.

There are a lot of surveys that talk about ranges for Day-to-Day compensation. Most surveys group people into grades and have ranges for the grades. Find the right categories for your employees. Don't have all the grades just because some survey looked at those grades.

> **96. Are your employees fairly compensated?**

Try to hire people into the middle to low end of the range for a grade so they can grow into the range and not be looking for a promotion to the next grade quickly. Pay less on the Day-to-Day salary and more on Retrospective rewards. Salaries are entitlements. The only reasonable way to take it away is to fire someone. Retrospective rewards should be based on behavior and actual accomplishments.

If you want accountability, tie Retrospective rewards to performance. In established companies where the hours are more regular and workloads are steadier, give bonuses to a subset of the organization (10%-30%) on a quarterly basis. Base the bonus on going above and beyond what your employee's day-to-day expectations were the previous quarters.

In smaller more aggressive environments, give bonuses to whole organizations based on meeting their schedules. You can make a cliff at 75% (i.e. if they didn't have a schedule or make at least 75% of their schedule, they got no bonus at all).

Usually some components of Retrospective Rewards are based on company wide or group-wide performance to encourage teamwork.

Finally Forward-Looking rewards give incentives to people to be part of the team and produce over the long haul. Rewards like stock options are multi-year things and unless you are close to IPO or your stock is jumping daily, they will have little influence on a daily basis. Many of us have plenty of stock and options that are worth nothing. You and your employees can make money on company stock but you should never misconstrue it as an immediate incentive because of its long-term nature. On the other hand, companies that are stingy with stock will not achieve the long-term incentives they desire.

Make ranges for all types of compensation per grade and stay within those ranges. If you have to make an exception to hire a superstar, try to make it occur in the Forward-Looking rewards or if needed in a one-time bonus. If you make exceptions to salaries, your team will be unbalanced with regard to compensation. That can cause complaints about fairness.

> 97. *Do your employees understand your compensation plan and what it takes for them to get rewarded or move up the ladder?*

As I said in the section on *Reviews*, take the time to make sure your employees know what it takes to be proficient in their current grade and what it takes to get to the next grade. Things like spheres of influence, self-management, and leadership are key differentiators.

Empathy

> 98. Do you have empathy for your employees?

It is easy to forget to be empathetic while in the process of doing business.

This is another area that has been a challenge for me personally. It is related to the issue above regarding making sure people feel heard.

> 99. Do you take the time to recognize your employees' feelings during conversations as opposed to just dealing with facts?

Even in the worst of situations, using empathy can help situations turn from disasters to successes. Whether you are talking about tough relationships or tough reviews or just prosecuting schedules, empathy helps.

One time, I gave my team a CD from Jim Faye[2] who is a teacher and lecturer on how to raise kids and handle difficult kids. He would say very clearly that if you do not hand out empathy along with consequences, the message would rarely be received. If you do not spend the time to acknowledge feelings and relate to those feelings, then it will be hard for people to relate to you and accept a reprimand or consequences.

Jim might give an example when he would get his child up extra early to complete a chore he forgot before he went to school that day. He would say something like: "I know I hate it when I have to get up early to finish work I forgot to do the night before. It must be really hard for you to have me get you up early to do the chores you forgot last night. Let's work together to make sure this does not happen again."

---

[2] Jim Faye, *Helicopters, Drills Sergeants and Consultants: parenting styles and the messages they send* (Golden, CO: The Love and Logic Institute, Inc., 1986).

As I mentioned earlier, at one company in which I worked we had hired a contractor to do product management for one of our products and he had a significant run-in with one of my managers. I joined in because it came down to some roles and responsibilities issues. Instead of being empathetic about what it must be like to be a contractor in that position, I made it worse by standing on ceremony. This caused a significant rift between the product management team and me.

When I was at Sun, I had to deal with a part of the company that was not working on mainstream products and wanted to break all sorts of rules to get their software into a Solaris release. We had to hold them off. In that case, I used the Jim Faye technique mentioned above and I will say that it was the best interaction I ever had with that group.

Chapter 11: Final Words

> 100. What are you doing to make yourself and the managers reporting to you better?

The content of this book represents the questions I have and would ask my software managers. A lot of the same items come up in job after job. I hope they are a help to you.

I think, however, that each job brings new challenges and new perspectives. I will repeat again that although many of the sections are exact and directive, you need to temper it with your personal experience and your current environment.

I hope that this helps you along your path.

A fellow developer once asked me how I had the guts to do the things I do: driving technology, projects, products, teams, etc. They felt they were afraid to speak up or take the lead. If you have read this book, you are either a leader or want to be. Have no fear – if you do what you think is good for your company and your people, it will lead you far and you will sleep at night.

Keep learning. Keep growing. Find more resources to help you be successful.

Thank you for reading.

Appendix: Project Example

This appendix is an example to present samples for some of the techniques described in the book. I will begin with an explanation of the scenario for the example and then provide samples of the following:

- Elevator pitch
- Owners
- Strategy
- Engineering budget
- Engineering criteria
- Engineering schedule

I could not pick an example from my past because of the level of detail into which I would have to go and the confidentiality requirements for those companies. Instead, I picked a project that I know is happening in an industry in which I have not worked. The project is to allow cell phones to use TCP/IP (Transmission Control Protocol/Internet Protocol) version 6 with Mobile support instead of WAP (Wireless Application Protocol) to connect to the Internet. TCP/IP is the ubiquitous protocol computers use to talk to the Internet.

In no way do I claim to have enough knowledge to say this is real, accurate, or complete. It is just a made-up example, so suspend belief for a short period of time and just take the example as is.

I will only provide subsets of samples of the documents for the project in this example due to the space and complexity of showing these examples in a book. I present enough for you to get a flavor of the techniques presented in this book. I am also including the sources files for the samples at www.heavenstone.us.

I present to you XYZZ Corporation who is a carrier for cell phone service in the United States They have had success in getting their customers to use the Internet on their phones and collecting monthly service charges for the service. Problems have arisen with using WAP for their customers because of reliability issues, scaling issues, and security issues. XYZZ would also like to take advantage of all the work being done for computers using the Internet via TCP/IP and use those same protocols for their cellular Internet service.

Elevator Pitch

The *Elevator Pitch* for XYZZ comes from their company slogan "At Your Fingertips". In the case of Wireless Internet this translates to the service always working well and the functions that the customer wants to be available.

Owners

The following are fictitious owners of specific parts of our project:

- Engineer and Productization   **Ken**
    - Ken will be responsible for the engineering contribution to the strategies that led up to the formation of this project. He also leads the line organization and will allocate resources and insure that cross-functional issues within engineering get resolved.
- Product Definition   **Morgan**
    - Morgan is Ken's counterpart in product management and together they drive the strategies. He will also drive the project plan and requirements documents. He will drive cross-functional coordination within the

company between engineering, support, sales, etc. Morgan's boss runs the steering committee which approves both strategies and project proposals.
- Server Software and Management Lead **John**
    - John runs the group doing the server software that will provide the TCP/IP service from the transceivers back to the servers that connect to the Internet. Ken has chosen John to be the management-lead for this project. This means he will own, with support from the program manager and tech lead, the schedules and the engineering input to the project proposal.
- Handset Software   **Gena**
    - Gena manages the handset software team, and her team is responsible for the protocol and applications that run on the handset.
- Quality Development   **Tony**
    - Tony manages the Quality development and test execution teams. Those teams will develop the integration test, a staging environment, and execute both the tests his team develops and the tests developed by engineering.
- Publications   **Arnold**
    - Arnold manages the Publications group; and his team will develop the documentation in the handset, a manual for the handset, a server operations guide so XYZZ's IT group can run the service, and localization for messages and documentation.
- Tech Lead   **Brenda**
    - Brenda is the overall tech lead for this project. She will be the one stop shop for technical information and decision making across the project from handset to server. While she is not expected to have every piece of information at her fingertips or make all decisions, she owns getting information as needed and getting the decisions made; she is empowered to make them if necessary.
- Program Manager   **Frank**
    - Frank owns all of the documents for the project you will see in this chapter. Frank produces and manages those documents. Frank makes

sure everyone has access to all of the information and helps coordinate meetings. Frank also produces status on a weekly basis for the project.

Budget Categories

XYZZ has developed the following top-down categories for their *Budget* for their wireless Internet service:

- Reliability
- Performance/Scalability
- Security
- Functionality
- Productization

Reliability refers to the customer's ability to connect to the service. Is the service up? Is it reachable? Is it usable? The company measures complaints about non-use and requests for refunds and cancellations due to reliability issues.

Performance and Scalability refers to the customer's experience using the product. How quickly do pages get presented? This is a combination of hardware and software. The system must be capable of adding on new customers, providing a lot of bandwidth, caching frequently used web pages, and optimizing the presentation of web pages.

Security refers to protecting the customer's private information including supporting safe password dialogues, encrypted communications, and protecting billing information.

Functionality refers to the features the phone provides. The basic functionality is web browsing but there are a lot of other features requested by customers and supplied by competitors. These include transcoding (making the webpages fit the cell phone screen better), Java support, providing TCP/IP applications other than web browsers (file transfer, remote machine access, etc.), document viewing (to see documents in Adobe PDF or Portable Document Format, Microsoft PowerPoint, etc.), email, calendaring, etc.

Productization refers to the integration, localization, testing, certification, release, and support processes. Some of these items actually get included in the other categories when the other categories drive a particular task: e.g. testing for a new feature.

Reliability Strategy

XYZZ Corporation has developed strategies for each of the categories listed above. I will share with you the Reliability strategy, as it is the main driver for this project in order to increase the reliability of the cellular Internet service for XYZZ's customers. But the Reliability strategy is not the only strategy supporting this project. This is normal. Other strategies may include this project for other reasons. For example, the Functionality strategy wants to move from WAP to TCP/IP because they can almost immediately add new applications and functionality that use the TCP/IP protocol.

The Project presentation, which I will present later in this appendix, will bring together all of the reasons for doing the project from the different strategies. This points out the fact that a project will naturally support multiple strategies. It also poses challenges when there are limited resources and not all of the work can be funded to support the goals of disparate strategies.

Here is the Reliability strategy:

Reliability Strategy

Morgan, Product Management

Ken, Engineering

Overview

- Taxonomy
- Competition
- Today
- Tomorrow
- Projects

Taxonomy

- TCP/IP
  - Handset, server
- Handset compatibility
  - How broad a set of handsets will we support?
- Field upgrade
  - Can you upgrade the software in the field easily?
- Scalability
  - How well does the system scale with both the number of handsets and volume of internet traffic?
- Performance
  - How fast can we load pages?
- User experience
  - Everything: performance, usability, readability, etc.
- Scripting
  - Java, HTML, etc.
- Continuous operation
  - Is the internet just on or is it a mode?

XYZZ Corporation
Proprietary and Confidential

Competition

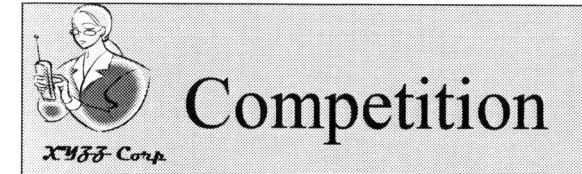

Taxonomy	XYZZ Today	XYZZ Tomorrow	DEF, Inc. next rev	HIJ, Ltd. next rev
TCP/IP	F	A	B	A
Compatibility	n/a	B	B	?
Field Upgrade	F	A	C	?
Scalability	C	A	B	A
Performance	C	B	B	A
User Experience	C	B	C	A
Scripting	C	A	C	A
Continuous Operation	F	A	A	A

XYZZ Corporation
Proprietary and Confidential

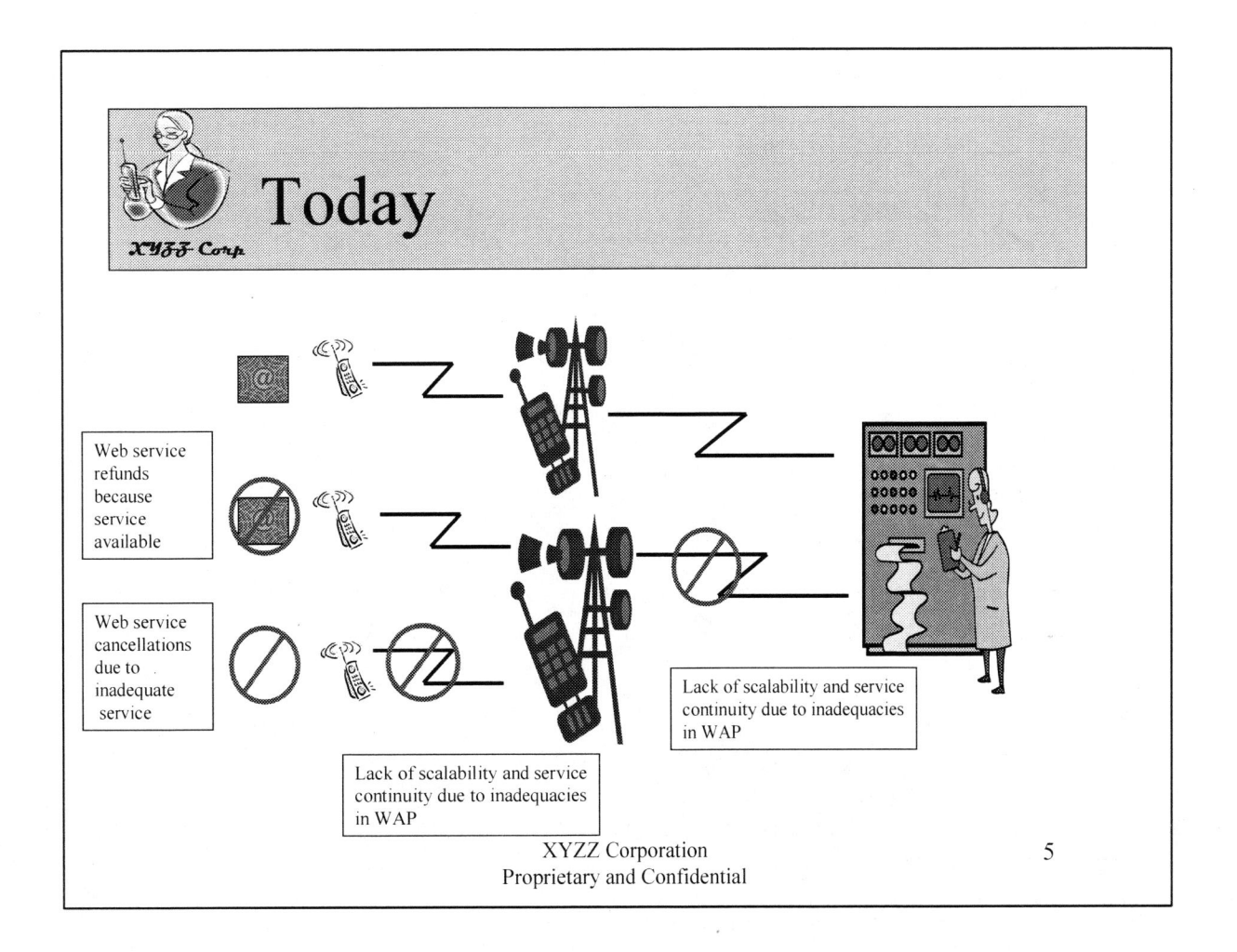

100 Questions to Ask Your Software Organization 117

Today

XYZZ Corp.

Web service refunds because service available

Web service cancellations due to inadequate service

Lack of scalability and service continuity due to inadequacies in WAP

Lack of scalability and service continuity due to inadequacies in WAP

XYZZ Corporation
Proprietary and Confidential

5

Tomorrow
XYZZ Corp.

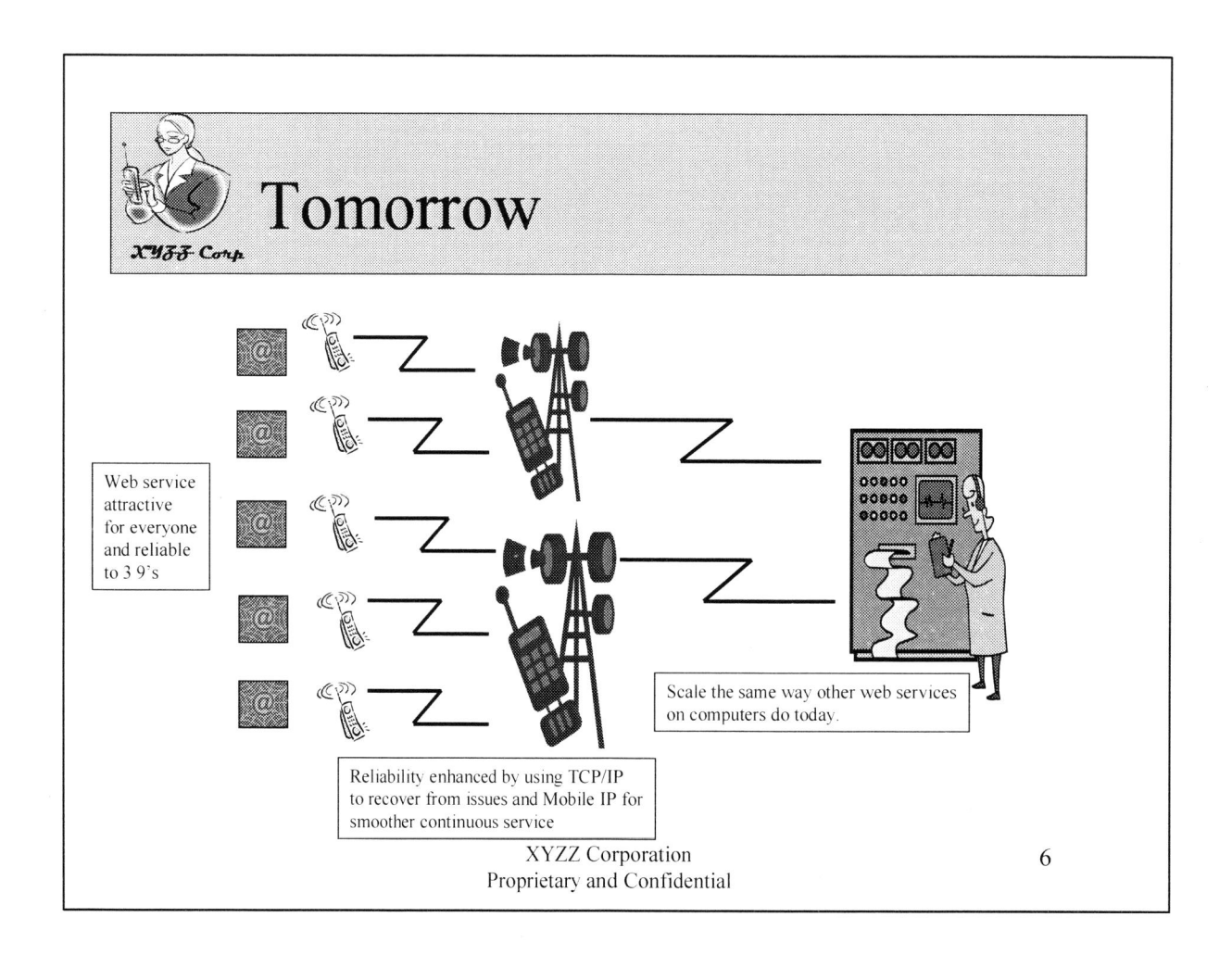

Web service attractive for everyone and reliable to 3 9's

Scale the same way other web services on computers do today.

Reliability enhanced by using TCP/IP to recover from issues and Mobile IP for smoother continuous service

Projects required

- TCP/IPV6/Mobile IP
  - Server
  - Handset
  - Browser
  - WAP coexistence/transition
- Phase II further performance and scalability improvements
  - Initial project lays the groundwork, this project increases capacity and throughput
- New branding/marketing program to entice old customers back and new customers to the service

Resources

- **TCP/IPV6/Mobile IP**
    - Headcount – X over 18 months
    - Test Equipment - $250,000
    - New deployment servers - $750,000
- **Phase II performance and scalability**
    - Headcount – 15 ongoing
- **Re-branding/Re-marketing**
    - Program Dollars - $1,000,000
    - Headcount – 5 over 12 months, 2 ongoing

Budgets

At some point in the process of planning the IPV6 project, a budget must be approved. This may actually happen before or after the strategy presentation. At this stage, the budget is somewhat of a guess and it must be calibrated later.

Sometimes it is hard for engineers to help produce a budget for which they have no engineering specification. You must help them. This requires a top level of definition and sizing for the project components. It also requires faith that management will adjust the boundaries of the project as necessary as more of the design progresses.

I will now present a spreadsheet with an engineering budget. Note that this is not a complete budget. A complete budget would have a lot more projects and features defined and the team would have to make more trade-offs. This budget would eventually be rolled up and reconciled with budgets from product management, product marketing, and support so that upper management could determine if the company is investing consistently. It is important that a project is funded for success from all parts of the company; otherwise, the company may be wasting money.

The spreadsheet is presented over two pages because it is too wide to present on one page. The columns on the left are repeated to make the spreadsheet easier to read. I have also included some Pivot Tables® that I will explain below. Here is the spreadsheet:

Appendix: Project Example

Organization	Owner	Project Name	Eng Priority	Product Mgt Priority	Sum Of Sqs Priority	Q1 Head count	...	Q4 Head count	Q1 Expenses in 1000s	...	Q4 Expenses in 1000s
Mgmt	Ken	Technical lead	10	10	200	1		1			
Mgmt	Ken	Program management	10	10	200	1		1			
Server	John	TCP/IPV6/mobileIP on server	7	10	149	4					
Handset	Gena	TCP/IPV6/mobileIP on handset	7	10	149	2					
Handset	Gena	Web browser on the cell phone	7	10	149	1					
Server	John	Webserver on server	7	10	149	1					
Server	John	Billing	7	10	149	1					
Handset	Gena	TCP/IP & WAP coexistence	7	10	149	0.5					
Handset	Gena	Configuration utility	7	10	149	0.5					
Pubs	Arnold	Online document	7	10	149			0.5			
Handset	Gena	Software update utility	7	10	149	0.5					
Server	John	Software update utility	7	10	149	0.5					
All	All	FCS Rollout support	7	10	149						
QA	Tony	End to end security testdev	7	10	149	3					100
All	All	Upgrade source code system	10	1	101	1					
All	All	Upgrade build tools	10	1	101	1					
Server	John	Scalability Phase I	7	7	98	3		3			
QA	Tony	End to end feature testdev	7	7	98	5			250		
QA	Tony	End to end performance testdev	7	7	98	2					
QA	Tony	End to end stress testdev	7	7	98	2					
QA	Tony	Test execution	7	7	98			6			
Pubs	Arnold	Localization	7	7	98			2			300
Pubs	Arnold	Handset documents	7	7	98			0.5			
Pubs	Arnold	Operations documents	7	7	98			0.5			
QA	Tony	Upgrade testdev	7	7	98	1					
All	All	Integration	7	7	98			20			
All	All	Alpha	7	7	98						
All	All	Beta	7	7	98						
Server	John	Performance	7	7	98	2		2			
Handset	Gena	Webserver transcoding	1	8	65	3		3			
Handset	Gena	Document viewing	1	8	65	3		3			
Handset	Gena	Handset VOIP	5	5	50	10		10			
Server	John	Server VOIP	5	5	50	10		10			
Server	John	Scalability Phase II	5	5	50			3			
Server	John	Quality of service	5	3	34	4		4			
Handset	Gena	Other TCP/IP applications	1	5	26	3		3			
Handset	Gena	Javascript support	1	5	26	1		1			
Handset	Gena	Continuous operation	1	3	10	2		2			
Total						69	0	75.5	250	0	400
Total for priority > 90						33	0	36.5	250	0	400

100 Questions to Ask Your Software Organization

Organization	Owner	Project Name	Category: Taxonomy	Category: Technology
Mgmt	Ken	Technical lead	productization	infrastructure
Mgmt	Ken	Program management	productization	infrastructure
Server	John	TCP/IPV6/mobileIP on server	reliability	protocol
Handset	Gena	TCP/IPV6/mobileIP on handset	reliability	protocol
Handset	Gena	Web browser on the cell phone	interface	browser
Server	John	Webserver on server	interface	browser
Server	John	Billing	productization	commerce
Handset	Gena	TCP/IP & WAP coexistence	productization	protocol
Handset	Gena	Configuration utility	interface	protocol
Pubs	Arnold	Online document	interface	publications
Handset	Gena	Software update utility	productization	installation
Server	John	Software update utility	productization	installation
All	All	FCS Rollout support	productization	maintenance
QA	Tony	End to end security testdev	productization	quality
All	All	Upgrade source code system	productization	infrastructure
All	All	Upgrade build tools	productization	infrastructure
Server	John	Scalability Phase I	scalability	protocol
QA	Tony	End to end feature testdev	productization	quality
QA	Tony	End to end performance testdev	productization	quality
QA	Tony	End to end stress testdev	productization	quality
QA	Tony	Test execution	productization	quality
Pubs	Arnold	Localization	productization	localization
Pubs	Arnold	Handset documents	interface	publications
Pubs	Arnold	Operations documents	interface	publications
QA	Tony	Upgrade testdev	productization	quality
All	All	Integration	productization	integration
All	All	Alpha	productization	integration
All	All	Beta	productization	integration
Server	John	Performance	scalability	protocol
Handset	Gena	Webserver transcoding	functionality	browser
Handset	Gena	Document viewing	functionality	browser
Handset	Gena	Handset VOIP	functionality	service
Server	John	Server VOIP	functionality	service
Server	John	Scalability Phase II	scalability	protocol
Server	John	Quality of service	scalability	protocol
Handset	Gena	Other TCP/IP applications	functionality	applications
Handset	Gena	Javascript support	functionality	browser
Handset	Gena	Continuous operation	functionality	browser
Total				
Total for priority > 90				

Pivot Table for Rollup by Taxonomy

	Data	
Category: Taxonomy	Sum of Q1 Headcount	Sum of Q4 Headcount
interface	2.5	1.5
productization	19.5	30
reliability	6	
scalability	5	5
Grand Total	33	36.5

Pivot Table for Rollup by Technology Area

	Data	
Category: Technology	Sum of Q1 Headcount	Sum of Q4 Headcount
browser	2	
commerce	1	
infrastructure	4	2
installation	1	
integration		20
localization		2
maintenance		
protocol	12	5
publications		1.5
quality	13	6
Grand Total	33	36.5

The spreadsheet does not have all the columns you might have, but it gives you a flavor of what a budget spreadsheet should look like.

I'd like to point out the following items in the spreadsheet:

- The "upgrading of the source code control system" task is a good example of what the sum of the squares does. Product management does not care how this is done but engineering does. Using the sum of the squares makes sure it does not disappear with other lower priority items.
- We have guessed that the project will take three calendar quarters of elapsed time but that needs corroboration when there is a schedule. We expect initial integration after code-freeze to occur in the fourth quarter. Developers move off development into integration. The quarterly budget numbers reflect these assumptions.
- XYZZ's budget dollars for this project will only pay for 35 developers. We included other projects below the line, which listed in the budget in the spreadsheet for future consideration.
- I include two pivot tables that roll up the costs by the categories we have defined. One is by the budget categories defined above and the other is by the technology associated with a budget item. The pivot tables provide investment profiles that can help companies decide if they are investing appropriate amounts in appropriate areas as discussed in the *Budget* section of the *Resources* chapter.

Project Proposal

The project proposal is the beginning of the definition process. A full product requirements document and engineering specification are required as well. A steering committee approval of the project proposal gives the teams permission to move forward. Here is the project proposal:

IPV6 Project Proposal

Morgan, Product Management
John, Engineering

Overview

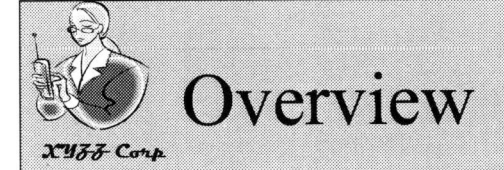

- What Is It?
- Business Case
- Features
- Quality
- Resources
- Schedules
- Issues/Challenges

What Is It?

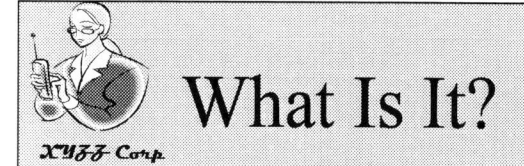

- Replace WAP with TCP/IPV6 and Mobile IP in Handsets for Internet Service. This requires work on the Server and Handset sides. Initially this will only be used for the Web Browser but it lays the foundation for taking advantage of all of the technology being developed for PCs that use TCP/IP including email, instant message, VOIP, etc.
- The Following strategies have proposed this project as part of their strategy: Reliability, Functionality, Performance/Scalability, and Security

Business Case

- Our Cancellation Rate is 35% for WAP-based internet service. 10% of Internet users changes carriers after service contracts are complete. If we reduce the churn by half over the next three years, we will see an increase in earnings of $300 million dollars.
- All of our major competition including DEF, Inc. and HIJ Ltd will have TCP/IP based solutions in the Next 24 months.
- Added services and applications built on top of this infrastructure could result in an additional total of $2 Billion in revenue from new and revamped products over the next 5 years. These products include email, instant messaging, and VOIP.

XYZZ Corporation
Proprietary and Confidential

Features

- Seamless transitioning from cell to cell.
- Increased availability of the service
  - Initially from the current 60% to 90%
- Increased performance of the service
  - up to double performance in key benchmarks
- Full support of SSL Pages
- Coexistence with WAP plus transition plan
- What is not included that might be expected:
  - Other non-browser applications (email, ftp, ssh, instant message, etc.), better transcoding, VOIP
- New Branding/Demand generation campaign
- Internationalized according to corporate standards

XYZZ Corporation
Proprietary and Confidential

Quality

- Be able to collect and meet all of the Quality related numbers for the *Criteria* document.
- Create new emulation environments and tests to test and drive traffic both to the handset and the servers. This will be used for stress, performance and scalability testing.
- End to End Security test development and third party certification.
- Pass existing test suites.
- Add to regression test suites as bugs come up in the development cycle.

Resources

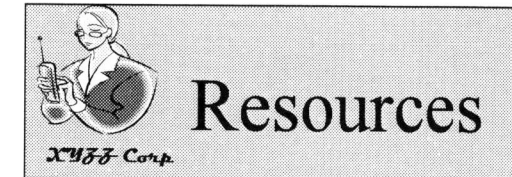

- Engineering
  - Headcount average   35
  - Headcount On Board Today   29
  - Expenses/Equipment $750,000
- Marketing
  - Headcount average   5
  - Headcount On Board Today   4
  - Expenses/Equipment $2,000,000
- Service
  - Expenses/Equipment $10,000,000

Schedules

- Initial Criteria, PRD & Specification — Q1
- Schedule Checkpoint 1 — Q1
  - full schedules available for review
- Schedule Checkpoint 2 — Q2
  - includes incomplete demonstrable product
- Code Freeze — Q4
- Launch Plan — Q4
- Service Deployment Plan — Q4
- Alpha — Q1 next year
- Beta — Q2 next year
- Launch/FCS — Q3/Q4 next year

Issues/Challenges

- Hitting window for Holiday Sales next year
- Complete transition plan from WAP
  - Cost of supporting both over time
- Handset support – which ones to test initially
- Coordination with the software release train

Notice the following things in the proposal:

- The proposal does not rehash the strategy. It assumes those are approved and everyone agrees to them. This proposal states the value of this project and how the team will accomplish it. It has context.
- The proposal makes clear what is being done and what is not being done.
- The proposal is not a product requirements review or an engineering specification review.
- The proposal makes it clear when the rest of the documentation that defines the project and its execution are due along with the delivery dates.

Criteria Document

The next document for our project is the Criteria document. This document will identify and collect measurements for all of the product goals. These goals must be met before the product is shipped.

The criteria document presented below represents one at some point in the middle of development. I did this so that you could see progress between different stages of development.

I broke the spreadsheet over two pages because it was too wide to fit on one. I repeated a number of columns in order to make it easier to read. Here is the Criteria document:

Section	Subsection	Owner	Where	Description	Unit Of Measure	Goal
Feature	Protocol	John	Server	IPV6	% complete	100
Feature	Protocol	Gena	Handset	IPV6	% complete	100
Feature	Browser	Gena	Handset	Web Broswer	% complete	100
Feature	Browser	John	Server	Web Server	% complete	100
Feature	Setup	Gena	Handset	Configuration Utility	% complete	100
Feature	Protocol	John	Server	Mobile IP	% complete	100
Feature	Security		System	SSL	% complete	100
Feature	Protocol	Gena	Handset	Mobile IP	% complete	100
Feature	Upgrade	Gena	Handset	Upgrade utility	% complete	100
Feature	Upgrade	John	Server	Upgrade server	% complete	100
Feature	Billing	John	Server	Billing	% complete	100
Feature	Localization	Gena	Handset	Localization	% complete	100
Feature	Documentation	Gena	Handset	Online Documentation	% complete	100
Feature	Documentation	Gena	Handset	Manual	% complete	100
Feature	Documentation	John	Server	Operations Manual	% complete	100
Testing	Unit	John	Server	Unit tests written	# written	500
Testing	Unit	Gena	Handset	Unit tests written	# written	200
Testing	Unit	John	Server	Unit tests run	# passed	500
Testing	Unit	Gena	Handset	Unit tests run	# passed	200
Testing	Interoperability	Tony	Handset	Nokia XXX	pass/fail	pass
Testing	Interoperability	Tony	Handset	Motorola XXX	pass/fail	pass
Testing	Interoperability	Tony	Handset	Ericsson XXX	pass/fail	pass
Testing	Stress	Tony	System	handsets per cell	# of handsets	200
Testing	Stress	Tony	System	handset cell associations	changes/minute/handset	20
Testing	Stress	Tony	System	throughput sustained	kbits/sec/handset	10
Testing	Stress	Tony	System	packet loss	% retransmit	5
Testing	Stress	Tony	System	concurrent updates	number	1000
Testing	Perfomance	Tony	System	indivudal handset	kbits/sec	20
Testing	Perfomance	Tony	System	50 handsets	kbits/sec	5
Testing	Wall clock	Tony	System	cell change delay	sec	1
Testing	Wall clock	Tony	System	yahoo page bringup	sec	5
Testing	Wall clock	Tony	System	google page bringup	sec	3
Quality	Bugs	Frank	System	P1 bugs	number	0
Quality	Bugs	Frank	System	Bugs/1000 lines of code	number	3
Quality	Bugs	Frank	System	trend of new P1s /week	number	1
Legal	Patents	Ken	System	patents	patents applied for	10
Legal	Copyrights	Ken	Internal	verify correct copyrights	yes/no	yes
Legal	Copyrights	Ken	External	display correct copyrights	yes/no	yes
Certification	Security	Tony	System	third party certification	pass/fail	pass
Certification	Export	Ken	System	us government export	yes/no	yes

100 Questions to Ask Your Software Organization

Section	Subsection	Goal	Baseline	Last Run	Current Run	Notes
Feature	Protocol	100	80	80	80	
Feature	Protocol	100	80	80	80	
Feature	Browser	100	50	75	75	
Feature	Browser	100	75	75	75	
Feature	Setup	100	10	50	50	
Feature	Protocol	100	0	80	80	
Feature	Security	100	0	0	50	
Feature	Protocol	100	0	80	80	
Feature	Upgrade	100	0	50	50	
Feature	Upgrade	100	0	50	50	
Feature	Billing	100	0	0	50	
Feature	Localization	100	0	0	0	
Feature	Documentation	100	0	0	0	
Feature	Documentation	100	0	0	0	
Feature	Documentation	100	0	0	0	
Testing	Unit	500	100	225	300	
Testing	Unit	200	25	95	125	
Testing	Unit	500	30	150	225	
Testing	Unit	200	10	75	100	
Testing	Interoperability	pass	not run	not run	pass	
Testing	Interoperability	pass	pass	pass	pass	
Testing	Interoperability	pass	not run	not run	not run	
Testing	Stress	200	10	100	100	50 webusers, 50 sustained calls, 25 initiating calls, 25 recieving calls, 25 terminating calls, 25 changing cells
Testing	Stress	20	3	15	15	200 phones, 3 cells, without losing service
Testing	Stress	10	1	5	7	200 phones
Testing	Stress	5	20	10	10	100 webusers, 5 kbits/sec
Testing	Stress	1000	10	100	100	update cell phone software
Testing	Performance	20	1	5	7	maximum
Testing	Performance	5	1	5	5	expected
Testing	Wall clock	1	3	3	3	
Testing	Wall clock	5	10	8	8	
Testing	Wall clock	3	7	6	6	
Quality	Bugs	0	76	42	35	
Quality	Bugs	3	10	7.5	7	
Quality	Bugs	1	30	30	30	
Legal	Patents	10	1	4	4	
Legal	Copyrights	yes	yes	yes	yes	
Legal	Copyrights	yes	no	yes	yes	
Certification	Security	pass	not run	not run	not run	
Certification	Export	yes	no	no	no	

The Criteria document has now gotten into fictitious detail about the project. The important concepts from that document are:

- Identify the major features and their status.
- Identify both the functional and integration tests and the product goals they represent. The integration tests will become input for the marketing collateral document for the product.
- Identify the quality status for the product.
- Identify some of the legal and certification pieces of the product.

Note that this document does not include the launch plan. This criteria document is only an engineering document. Product management must have a similar document for a launch plan that includes support and field readiness, collateral, analyst and press tours, advertisement, demand generation, etc.

Remember that this document would be more elaborate in a real world situation.

Schedule

I will present a portion of the schedule. I will include some major milestones and two features: the update application and service and the handset configuration application.

The update application and service provides the ability for customers to update the software on their cell phone the same way one might do this on a personal computer. This is critical because the team expects customers to want bug fixes and enhancements and new features after the product is sold. The team feels that if they do not make these seamless and easy, users might not update their software. This would impact the customer's feeling about the quality of the service and limit XYZZ's ability to sell them new features.

The configuration utility will only be used by expert users and users who experience problems and are working with XYZZ's support team. This will behave very much like a control panel on a personal computer for networking settings.

There are two developers introduced in this schedule subset. The first is Casey and she works in John's group on the server side of the update application. Her work includes defining the package or payload sent from the server down to the handset, the service which will respond to update requests and the scalability of that service.

The second developer is Tom. Tom is the lead for both the update project and configuration utility project. He is also responsible for developing the software that runs on the handset. There will be an application that a handset customer will run to use each of these applications. Tom is in Gina's group, and he works closely with Casey and the technical lead, Brenda, to complete the designs and integrate this part of the product.

Note that if either of these projects got large, they might require their own project proposals. Project proposals can contain projects that require their own proposals. If the update application and service required a project proposal, the team would first get the whole project approved and then get this subproject approved. This natural hierarchy allows for more or less process as needed.

Note that I used Microsoft® Project as the tool in this sample, but it may seem that I use it differently than others you may have seen before. Rather than using it as a task centric tool, I typically create one task per individual and one task for each subproject and then create dependencies to tie the developers together with deliverables. This technique makes it easier to see the hierarchical nature of projects and manage resources more clearly.

I have included both the task list and a Gantt chart which is a graphical illustration using bars to depict schedule tasks and dependencies. I created a custom column in Microsoft Project to identify the subproject to which a task is assigned since I organize by resource rather than tasks (see above).

I copied the task sheet into a spreadsheet and cleaned up some of the entries. The task sheet is long enough that it spans two pages. I have included images of the Gantt charts over two pages as well but they may still be too small for some readers to see. As stated above, For a limited time, I will post source copies of these documents at www.heavenstone.us.

Here is the task sheet and Gantt chart for our schedule:

100 Questions to Ask Your Software Organization

Task #	Feature	Task Name	Duration in Days	Start	Finish	Dependencies	Resource
1	resource	Casey		01/02/06	03/21/07		
2	update	start		01/02/06	01/02/06		Casey
3	update	server design document	5	01/02/06	01/09/06	2	Casey
4	update	library to create update package	3	01/10/06	01/12/06	3,15	Casey
5	update	library to unpack update package	4	01/16/06	01/19/06	4	Casey
6	update	update service	6	01/10/06	01/18/06	3	Casey
7	update	service and handset integration	5	01/26/06	02/06/06	34	Casey
8	update	service scalability	10	02/06/06	02/22/06	7	Casey
9	update	code freeze bug fixing	10	09/18/06	10/03/06	60	Casey
10	update	alpha bug fixing	5	12/11/06	12/18/06	62	Casey
11	update	beta bug fixing	5	03/13/07	03/21/07	63	Casey
12							
13	resource	Tom		01/03/06	03/20/07		
14	update	start		01/03/06	01/03/06		Tom
15	update	client design document	5	01/03/06	01/09/06	14	Tom
16	update	package download	4	01/10/06	01/13/06	3,15	Tom
17	update	update utility	7	01/16/06	01/24/06	16	Tom
18	update	partial update recovery	8	01/16/06	01/25/06	16	Tom
19	update	service and handset integration	5	01/26/06	02/02/06	34	Tom
20	update	code freeze bug fixing	10	09/15/06	09/29/06	60	Tom
21	update	alpha bug fixing	5	12/08/06	12/15/06	62	Tom
22	update	beta bug fixing	5	03/13/07	03/20/07	63	Tom
23	configuration	start		01/09/06	01/09/06	15	Tom
24	configuration	client design document	5	01/10/06	01/16/06	23	Tom
25	configuration	main configuration screen	8	02/02/06	02/14/06	24,19	Tom
26	configuration	advanced configuration screen	8	02/14/06	02/24/06	25	Tom
27	configuration	client/server integration	10	09/01/06	09/15/06	42,50	Tom
28	configuration	code freeze bug fixing	2	09/15/06	09/19/06	60	Tom
29	configuration	alpha bug fixing	2	12/08/06	12/12/06	62	Tom
30	configuration	beta bug fixing	2	03/13/07	03/15/07	63	Tom
31							
32	project	update		01/03/06	03/21/07		

Task #	Feature	Task Name	Duration in Days	Start	Finish	Dependencies	Resource
33	update	start		01/03/06	01/03/06	2,14	update
34	update	code complete		01/26/06	01/26/06	6,18	update
35	update	integration complete		02/06/06	02/06/06	7,19	update
36	update	performance and bug fixing		10/04/06	10/04/06	9,20	update
37	update	alpha bug fixing		12/19/06	12/19/06	10,21	update
38	update	beta bug fixing		03/21/07	03/21/07	11,22	update
39							
40	project	configuration		01/10/06	03/15/07		
41	configuration	start		01/10/06	01/10/06	23	configuration
42	configuration	code complete		02/24/06	02/24/06	26	configuration
43	configuration	integration complete		09/15/06	09/15/06	27	configuration
44	configuration	code freeze bug fixing		09/19/06	09/19/06	28	configuration
45	configuration	alpha bug fixing		12/12/06	12/12/06	29	configuration
46	configuration	beta bug fixing		03/15/07	03/15/07	30	configuration
47							
48	project	ipv6 protocol		01/02/06	11/20/06		
49	protocol	start		01/02/06	01/02/06		protocol
50	protocol	code complete		09/01/06	09/01/06	49	protocol
51	protocol	integration complete		09/13/06	09/13/06	50	protocol
52	protocol	code freeze bug fixing		10/16/06	10/16/06	51	protocol
53	protocol	alpha bug fixing		11/20/06	11/20/06	52	protocol
54	protocol	beta bug fixing		11/20/06	11/20/06	53	protocol
55	protocol	fcs bug fixing		11/20/06	11/20/06	54	protocol
56							
57	product	milestones		01/10/06	03/21/07		
58	product	start		01/10/06	01/10/06	33,41,49	product
59	product	schedule update 1		01/17/06	01/17/06	3,15,24	product
60	product	code freeze		09/15/06	09/15/06	34,42,50	product
61	product	cross project integration	6 wks	09/15/06	10/27/06	60	product
62	product	alpha	6 wks	10/27/06	12/08/06	61,36,44,52	product
63	product	beta	12 wks	12/19/06	03/13/07	62,37,45,53	product
64	product	fcs		03/21/07	03/21/07	63,38,46,54	product

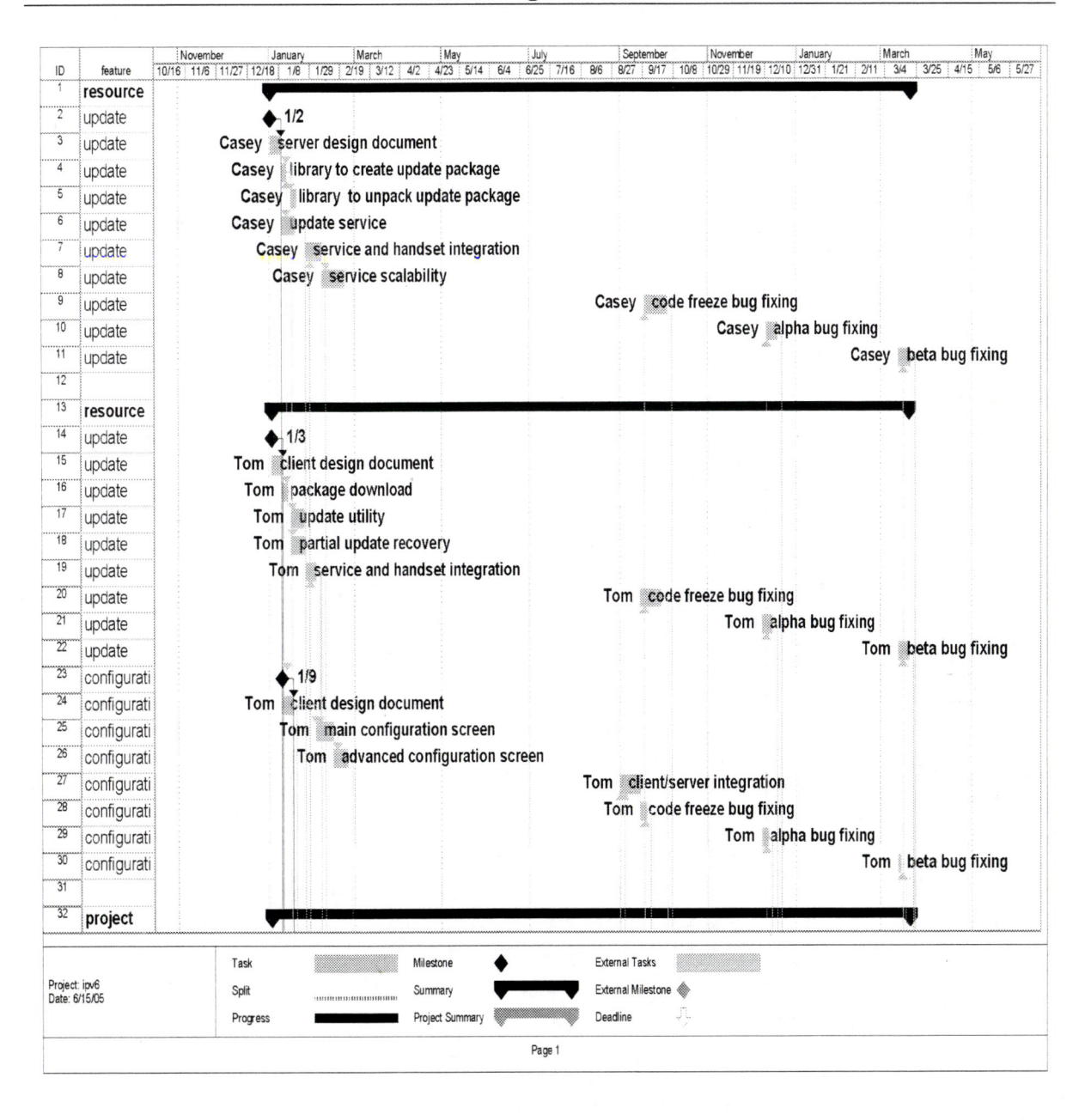

100 Questions to Ask Your Software Organization

ID	feature	Schedule
1	resource	
2	update	◆ 1/2
3	update	Casey server design document
4	update	Casey library to create update package
5	update	Casey library to unpack update package
6	update	Casey update service
7	update	Casey service and handset integration
8	update	Casey service scalability
9	update	Casey code freeze bug fixing
10	update	Casey alpha bug fixing
11	update	Casey beta bug fixing
12		
13	resource	
14	update	◆ 1/3
15	update	Tom client design document
16	update	Tom package download
17	update	Tom update utility
18	update	Tom partial update recovery
19	update	Tom service and handset integration
20	update	Tom code freeze bug fixing
21	update	Tom alpha bug fixing
22	update	Tom beta bug fixing
23	configurati	◆ 1/9
24	configurati	Tom client design document
25	configurati	Tom main configuration screen
26	configurati	Tom advanced configuration screen
27	configurati	Tom client/server integration
28	configurati	Tom code freeze bug fixing
29	configurati	Tom alpha bug fixing
30	configurati	Tom beta bug fixing
31		
32	project	

Project: ipv6
Date: 6/15/05

Task
Split
Progress
Milestone
Summary
Project Summary
External Tasks
External Milestone
Deadline

Appendix: Project Example

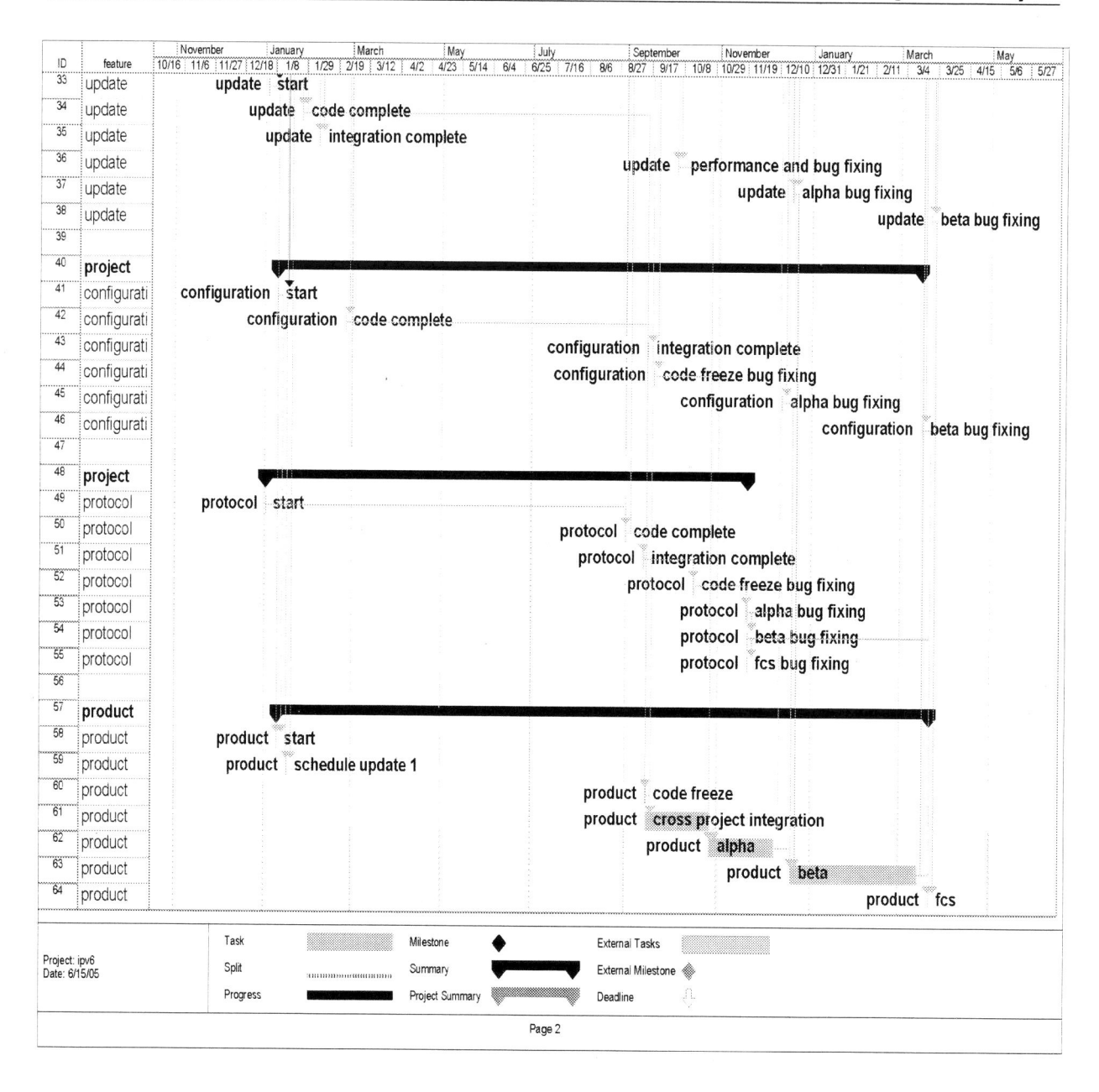

ID	feature	Schedule
33	update	update start
34	update	update code complete
35	update	update integration complete
36	update	update performance and bug fixing
37	update	update alpha bug fixing
38	update	update beta bug fixing
39		
40	**project**	
41	configurati	configuration start
42	configurati	configuration code complete
43	configurati	configuration integration complete
44	configurati	configuration code freeze bug fixing
45	configurati	configuration alpha bug fixing
46	configurati	configuration beta bug fixing
47		
48	**project**	
49	protocol	protocol start
50	protocol	protocol code complete
51	protocol	protocol integration complete
52	protocol	protocol code freeze bug fixing
53	protocol	protocol alpha bug fixing
54	protocol	protocol beta bug fixing
55	protocol	protocol fcs bug fixing
56		
57	**product**	
58	product	product start
59	product	product schedule update 1
60	product	product code freeze
61	product	product cross project integration
62	product	product alpha
63	product	product beta
64	product	product fcs

Project: ipv6
Date: 6/15/05

Task — Milestone ♦ — External Tasks
Split — Summary — External Milestone
Progress — Project Summary — Deadline

Page 2

The schedule should be monitored and updated on a regular basis. Microsoft Project and other tools allow you to enter percent complete and find out the days left. Schedules are living documents. You must remember what was originally promised but you must adjust as appropriate. If you make changes to the milestones, then the change would have to be approved as appropriate.

I hope this example helps solidify some of the concepts presented earlier in the book.

Index of Questions

Chapter 1: Communication *1*
No Surprises **2**
1. Do you get critical information in a timely manner? 2
2. Have you established a culture that encourages addressing tough issues? 3
3. Do people surprise you outside your organization with information regarding your organization that you did not know? 5

Escalations **5**
4. Have you established clear escalation paths and processes? 5
5. Have you made it clear when to escalate a problem? 7

Rationale **8**
6. Do you share the rationale for your decisions with your employees? 8

Venues **9**
7. Have you established regular meetings with different constituencies in your organization? 9
8. Do you have a communication plan? 11

Consensus **11**
9. Do you take the time to bring key stakeholders into the decision process? 11
10. Do you develop communication plans when you are rolling out big announcements or changes? 12

Messages and Rules **12**
11. Do you communicate goals and consequences along with rules? 12

Managing Up **17**
12. Do you take the time to communicate with upper management? 17

Chapter 2: Roles and Responsibilities *19*
One Owner **20**

    13. Have you identified one and only one owner for projects, products, tasks, etc?..20

Matrix Organizations..**22**
    14. Have you identified cross-functional organizations and reporting structures?22
    15. Have you developed mechanisms to authorize people running cross-functional organizations to succeed?...24

Steering..**25**
    16. Have you established cross-functional teams to define and drive your products and projects?..25

Program Management..**27**
    17. Do you have program managers and have you identified their responsibilities?...27

Quality Assurance..**29**
    18. Have you established how your organization will do quality assurance and who is responsible for it?..29

Information vs. Decisions...**30**
    19. Do you achieve the balance in your organizations to both allow a free flow of information and identify the owners of decisions?.................................30

Delegation..**32**
    20. Have you established what decisions you are willing to delegate and what decisions need to be finalized through you?..32

Accountability..**33**
    21. Have you developed mechanisms to determine when people and teams are off course?..33

Identifying Roles...**34**
    22. Have you identified the roles in your organization and who is responsible for those roles?...34

Separation..**36**
    23. Do you and your managers behave in a way that differentiates them from developers?...36
    24. Do you and your managers respect the privacy of their employees?............37

Chapter 3: Strategy..***39***
    Engineer's Lament..**40**

    25. Do you and your team believe the strategy? 40
Elevator Pitch **41**
    26. Does your company have a strategy that is easy to articulate? 41
Context and Organization **42**
    27. Do you have processes that allow your strategy to both scale and remain consistent within your company? 42
    28. Can you and your team articulate the strategy? 42
    29. Have you developed templates that provide disparate projects and products a way to present the data for their strategies in common terms agreed to by your company? 43
    30. Do you have processes in place to map the strategy to a roadmap? 46

Chapter 4: Resources *47*
  Budgets **48**
    31. Do you have a well-defined budget process? 48
    32. Do you have a list of what each person is working on? 49
    33. Do you have a list of the projects and products your company wants you and your team to work on and a mechanism for prioritizing those products? 50
    34. Do you have a mechanism for modifying the list of projects and products your team is working on after the initial budgeting process is complete? 52
  Hiring **52**
    35. Do you have a process for measuring, managing, and succeeding at hiring? 52
    36. Have you taken the steps to make hiring a priority for you and your team? .. 53
    37. Do you and your team have processes in place to make newly hired developers successful? 56
  Layoffs **56**
    38. Do you have the processes and plans in place in case your company needs to layoff people in your organization? 56

Chapter 5: Schedules *58*
  Form versus Function **59**
    39. Do you require schedules for all of your developers? 59
    40. If your employees meet their schedules, can they go home at the end of the week knowing they have done a good job and completed their tasks or do they feel they need to keep working regardless? 59

41. Have you identified all of the dependencies in your schedules (inside your group, inside your company, and outside your company)?	59
42. Do you have a mechanism for managing the schedule once it is initially complete?	60
43. Do you have an agreed upon tool for developing and managing schedules?	60

Granularity and Milestones **61**

44. Is the granularity of your schedules fine grain enough to give you early warning when your team is off-course?	61
45. Have you identified the key milestones for your schedules and deliverables required to make those milestones?	61
46. Does your schedule have discreet deliverables that enable you to determine that a task in a schedule is both complete and correct?	63
47. Do you have buy-in from your developers for their schedules?	64
48. Have you communicated the schedule throughout the company?	64

Chapter 6: Execution **66**

Auditing progress **67**

49. Do you have a process to manage when a project or product goes off course?	67
50. Do you have a mechanism to track why your projects and products go off course?	68
51. Have you identified who is responsible for tracking status of products and projects?	69

Continuous Improvement **69**

52. Do you have a process for improving your organization based on ongoing experience?	69

Marketing Yourself and Your Group **71**

53. Do you communicate both success and failures to your key stakeholders on a regular basis?	71
54. Have you identified the key stakeholders for your product or project?	72

Chapter 7: Development Processes **74**

Processes **75**

55. Do you have a well-defined set of processes for development so new developers can succeed quickly?	75

100 Questions to Ask Your Software Organization

- 56. Do your development processes account for exceptional situations? 75
- **Criteria** **76**
  - 57. Do you have well defined criteria for accepting a product at each stage of development? 76
- **Source code control** **78**
  - 58. Do you have a single source code control tool? 78
  - 59. Do you have processes and tools that help you manage multiple simultaneous releases? 79
  - 60. Do you have processes that minimize regressions from release to release? 79
  - 61. Do you have processes and tools that can limit changes to a product as you get close to release? 79
- **Release Models** **80**
  - 62. Do you have a train based release model? 80
- **Managing Bugs** **81**
  - 63. Do you have a bug management tool in your company? 81
  - 64. Does your bug tracking system allow you to express the severity of the bug, when it needs to be fixed, and what the customer thinks is the importance of the bug? 82
  - 65. Do you have tools and processes in place that help you manage bug trends and rates? 83

Chapter 8: Remote Management *85*
- **Why Do It?** **86**
  - 66. Have you identified why are you doing remote management? 86
  - 67. Do you have a communication plan in place for remote sites? 86
  - 68. Do you support extensive travel between sites? 87
- **Center of Gravity** **87**
  - 69. Have you created teams that integrate developers from your remote site and your main corporate site? 87
- **Care and Feeding** **88**
  - 70. Does your remote team feel like they are a valued part of the company? 88
  - 71. Is there a manager at your remote sites that can help local developers even if the developers do not report to them? 89
- **How to Do It** **89**

72. Do you have technical and managerial leadership at the remote site? 89
73. Do you have plans to provide challenging work for your remote team? 90
74. Is your company committed to having remote sites? 90
75. Do you have effective tools for communications and development at remote sites? 90
76. Do you measure the effectiveness and track issues with remote sites? 91
77. Have you allocated enough time and resources to train your team? 91
78. Who is the executive sponsor for your remote site? 91

Chapter 9: Offshoring 92
Why Do It? 93
79. Have you identified why you are doing development offshore? 93
80. If you have not started offshore development, have you done a cost/benefit analysis and looked at alternatives? 93
81. Have you identified who at your corporate site will be responsible for that team's success? 94

Chapter 10: Humanity 95
Make Them Feel Heard 96
82. Do your employees feel that you listen to them? 96
83. Do you employ techniques to ensure that employees know you understand their points of view? 96

Accomplishment 97
84. Do your employees feel accomplished? 97
85. Do you acknowledge your employees on a regular basis both in private and in public? 98

Reviews 98
86. Do you and your organization do reviews on time? 98
87. Do your reviews contain concrete examples? 98
88. Do you get peer feedback for your employee's reviews? 99
89. Do your reviews stress interaction skills enough (versus technical skills)? 100
90. Do you follow through on tough messages in reviews when necessary? ... 100

Success 101
91. Does your company feel like your employees are successful, and do you and your company make your employees feel successful? 101

Do the Right Thing **101**
    92.   Do you accommodate special situations for good employees? 101
    93.   Do you behave compassionately? 102
Compensation **102**
    94.   Do you have a well-defined compensation plan? 102
    95.   Do you differentiate between compensation that is meant as a reward for the past, ongoing remuneration for the present, and incentives for the future? 103
    96.   Are your employees fairly compensated? 103
    97.   Do your employees understand your compensation plan and what it takes for them to get rewarded or move up the ladder? 104
Empathy **105**
    98.   Do you have empathy for your employees? 105
    99.   Do you take the time to recognize your employees' feelings during conversations as opposed to just dealing with facts? 105

Chapter 11: Final Words ***107***
    100. What are you doing to make yourself and the managers reporting to you better? 107

Acknowledgments

Great thanks to all the people who reviewed this book: Sandra Himelstein, Tony Barreca, Leeaundra Temescu, Ike Nassi, Ken Matusow, Larry Weber, Carol Muratore, Robert Goosey, Ain McKendrick, Vivian Golub, Tim Weingarten, Matt Foley, Neal Kuhn, Chris Brennan, Barry Cooks, and Peter Cooper-Ellis.

Great love to my family for their everlasting patience and support.

About The Author

Mark Himelstein has been managing software organizations since 1984. He has led both small and large organizations in startups and Fortune 500™ companies. Mark's experience running the worldwide Solaris engineering group at Sun Microsystems, Inc. helped solidify some of the concepts found in this book. He also draws from experience running his own companies. Mark is currently the President and CEO of Heavenstone, Inc. a software development and management consulting firm (www.heavenstone.us).

Mark earned a Bachelor of Science in both Computer Science and Mathematics from Wilkes College in Wilkes-Barre, Pennsylvania. Mark earned his Masters in Computing Science from the University of California at Davis/Livermore. Mark holds four patents and has published a number of technical papers.

Mark lives in Saratoga, CA with his daughter Sammi.